What People Are Saying About

Divine

CW01501595

As someone who loves godde
healing, *Divine Wounds* is a
deep dive into many goddess
but powerful allies in healing nonetheless. Deep and fascinating
insights are given about goddesses such as Macha, Arianrhod
and Hera. Given the current state of our world, this book is a
timely addition to the Moon Books collection. The activities and
spells presented in this book offer impactful ways for healing
deep wounds that can hold us back. I would highly recommend
this anthology to anyone who wants to learn more about strong
goddess archetypes and/or seeks to form deep connections with
goddesses who exemplify the concept of sovereignty.

Robin Corak, author of *Dream Magick, Persephone,* and *Demeter*

Divine Wounds sets itself apart as an exploration of the journey
of the sacred feminine from wounding and death to healing
and re-claiming personal power. The stories in this anthology,
showcase the enduring spirit of women rising again and again,
unabated, to stand up to oppression, abuse and injustice
preponderant in male-dominated societies. These are stories
of pain, tears, and succumbing or begrudgingly submitting
to oppressors. These stories are also of resilience and victory,
casting women not as victims but heroes who continue to teach
and inspire. The contributors to this anthology went beyond
telling or re-interpreting myths, old or new. They went beyond
sharing their personal experience with pain. Through this book,
they generously offer their own wisdom and insight along with
well-thought practices to assist healing of wounded souls. To
admit to one's own vulnerability becomes thus the ultimate

proof of inner strength. Owning the personal narrative is the first step toward healing the wounded soul; then, sharing the story with others becomes both liberating and empowering. My debt of gratitude to the contributors of this beautiful anthology.
Daniela Simina, author of *Where Fairies Meet, A Fairy Path,* and *Fairy Herbs for Fairy Magic*

This beautiful volume brings together stories of Goddesses across cultures, told through a diversity of author voices, to provide both a balm for our sacred wounds and a roadmap to healing. Through storytelling, poetry, and personal reflection, each author demonstrates how Goddess imagery and Goddess spirituality can be a powerful tool for healing both our own wounds and those handed down through the generations. Suggestions for ritual, embodied practice, and exploration help readers take the next steps in their own healing. Beautiful, thoughtful, and important work between these covers!
Susan Harper, PhD, author of *Feminist Craft*

Ancient stories are weaved into modern practice through embracing the goddesses and all that they teach. An inspiring read that empowers us through the feminine.
Hannah Semple, Editor in Chief, *Pagan Dawn* magazine

Divine Wounds

Finding Healing by Working with
Goddesses and Archetypes

Divine Wounds

Finding Healing by Working with
Goddesses and Archetypes

Edited by Ness Bosch

MOON
BOOKS

London, UK
Washington, DC, USA

CollectiveInk

First published by Moon Books, 2025
Moon Books is an imprint of Collective Ink Ltd.,
Unit 11, Shepperton House, 89 Shepperton Road, London, N1 3DF
office@collectiveinkbooks.com
www.collectiveinkbooks.com
www.moon-books.net

For distributor details and how to order please visit the 'Ordering' section on our website.

Text copyright: Ness Bosch 2024

ISBN: 978 1 80341 507 9
978 1 80341 986 2 (ebook)
Library of Congress Control Number: 2024948921

All rights reserved. Except for brief quotations in critical articles or reviews, no part of this book may be reproduced in any manner without prior written permission from the publishers.

The rights of Ness Bosch as editor have been asserted in accordance with the Copyright, Designs and Patents Act 1988.

A CIP catalogue record for this book is available from the British Library.

Design: Lapiz Digital Services
Cover Artwork: The Tarot for the Sidhe. Dreamer 3 Card. Emily Carding. 2010. Schiffer.

UK: Printed and bound by CPI Group (UK) Ltd, Croydon, CR0 4YY
US: Printed and bound by Thomson-Shore, 7300 West Joy Road, Dexter, MI 48130

We operate a distinctive and ethical publishing philosophy in all areas of our business, from our global network of authors to production and worldwide distribution.

Contents

Honoring the women
of my lineage. And for every
Woman-Goddess that carries
a wound inflicted by the patriarchy…

Acknowledgements

This book is a tribute to the women in my family, especially my mother, who spent so many years suffering from her multiple wounds and illness. To my grandmothers and my cousins, Maritere and Noemi, for being there.

To the women who came into my life to share their love, strength and teachings with me despite there being no blood ties, to my dear Sophie and my "Comadre" Amalia. Thank you for the support and sorority over the years.

To Medusa and the Goddesses who are part of my life, Hekate, Hathor, Sulis, Clota, Agrona, Sekhmet, Astarte, Cailleach, Arianrhod and the other Goddesses who allow me to get closer to them to learn and heal.

To my editor Trevor Greenfield, Moon Books and Collective Ink for allowing me to share this idea. To each of the women who have participated by sharing in this anthology; Morgan, Tiffany, Halo, Isa, Victoria, Sian, Irisanya, Monica, Anwynn, Lindsay, Rachel, Frances and Mael. Thank you, Emily Carding, for allowing me to use your Dreamer 3 artwork from the Tarot of the Sidhe for our Cover.

And yes, there are many more stories to tell but maybe we can start with these.

The Heart of Dream is Torn in 3,
Leaving a hole where the whole should be,
The blessed Ravens feast on sorrow,
That the light might bring a fairer morrow...
Emily Carding

Foreword

Morgan Daimler

For many people drawn to pagan spirituality the stories of the gods act as guides and lessons. They are looked to for help in finding the right paths forward and for lessons in what not to do. But one aspect of divine stories that can be overlooked is the hope they may offer to those struggling through impossibly difficult situations, through abuse and betrayal. Perhaps it's because we don't want to see the gods as beings who deal with such human things or perhaps it's because we prefer the idea of our gods as strong and powerful and we find the idea of them being victimized too contradictory. But there is a wealth of stories of deities, especially goddesses, who are faced with and overcome the same things that humans suffer through and these stories too have immense value.

When we look at tales of goddesses who have endured trials and tribulations that are all too familiar in the human world – cheating spouses, betrayed promises, abandonment, physical abuse – we can find both comfort and strength. Knowing that the deities who we worship can relate to our pain makes them seem closer and more involved in our lives, and it makes them seem relatable. It bridges the gap between mortal and immortal, between the weak and the powerful, between human and divine. When a child dies, we feel our whole world has been broken, and Brighid understands that, having lost her son and mourned him. When we struggle to find justice in a world that seek to deny us, Áine understands that, having been raped by a king and then exacted revenge on her rapist so that he would lose his kingdom. When we are dealing with rumours and jealousy, Etaine understands that, a goddess who was forced out of her home – out of her physical form – by the jealousy of another.

When a loved one betrays us by breaking vital promises, Macha understands that, having lost her chosen home and husband to a broken promise. Everywhere we look we find deities who have been where we are now, who can empathize with our suffering, and whose stories can help us to feel less alone.

The examples I've given so far are all from Irish mythology as that's my own personal focus, but this book looks further afield than just that. From Branwen to Hera or Sulis, *Divine Wounds* explores the depths and power to be found when we open ourselves up to the stories of goddesses who have been in our situations, who have bled and suffered and cried as we do, who despite being so powerful have been put into situations where they were powerless – and overcome those situations one way or another. Their stories are our touchstones, reminding us that the last gift in Pandora's box was hope, and that hope is ultimately the greatest gift. Hope gives us the strength to push forward to keep fighting, whether it's the hope of change or the hope of justice, or the hope of freedom, or the hope of finding peace. Hope is the lesson in all the stories of these goddesses, in the end, because these stories show us that we too can get through what we must. They guide us into a better tomorrow.

Dealing with trauma is too often a lonely thing, an isolating thing, and a key to healing is breaking free of that feeling of isolation that cages us. We are not always in a position to share our own stories – sometimes we are still in the middle of their creation – but we can experience the stories of divine beings and see in them a reflection of ourselves. We can find comfort in sharing in the tales of these goddesses, no matter how painful, because it shows us that we are not alone, we are never alone, no matter how alone we may feel. Others have endured what we are enduring and while it can be painful to read of the goddess or goddesses we love being traumatized it creates a connection with them. When we pray to a deity knowing that deity has also experienced in stories what we are experiencing in life there is a feeling that they are listening and they understand. However abstract human life is in contrast to the life of goddesses, they understand.

Stories are powerful things. They shape our understanding of the world and of ourselves. Stories can harm us or they can help us, just as other living humans can, and by choosing to embrace stories of goddesses who have suffered we are both humanizing the gods and empowering ourselves. We are telling ourselves that yes, bad things happen but that survival and success are possible afterwards. These goddesses are part of entire tapestries of stories that weave together to help us, to guide us forward, to show us how things can be. We are standing in the middle of our own tales but being in it that middle feels like an end point, the furthest we have gotten – looking to these examples shows us what can be in the future, what healing and overcoming might look like. They show us possibilities beyond our own current pain, and they speak to what generations and millennia of people have already experienced. We are not alone, and there is hope.

This book is about stories, and about real-world trauma, and it is about connecting to those things in ways that help move us beyond their limits. Read of a goddess who has gone through what you are going through. Find a prayer to her that resonates with your own experiences or needs. Enact a ritual to create a deeper connection. Find healing. Start to find peace.

Preface

Ness Bosch

Finding empowerment in working with ancient gods is not new. The gods call us to their side for many reasons, to learn from them, so that we can know them. Sometimes this approach to the deity is born from a wound. The wound as a catalyst of consciousness, which opens windows to other realities and invisible worlds. It was a wound that directed me to approach Arianrhod. I embraced her wounds and mine in a moment of personal catharsis, she held me. I delved into the shadows of her story to understand my own wounds and found new strength walking alongside her.

That experience of working with Arianrhod led to bringing together different women, healing, wounds, deities, and archetypes in these pages. You are going to notice Welsh Goddesses are very present in the anthology. I see it as a sign that their stories have a lot of healing to share.

My journey with Arianrhod started in 2022, when I found myself deeply wounded from a relationship. With her help I managed not to drown, to find understanding and the energy to carry on. So, I owe her a lot. I wrote my essay as a way to honour her, while I was still internally bleeding from my wounds, and tried to expose some of the shadow of her story. I knew it was important to share this side of the Goddess, no matter what. I'm tired of seeing how some circles still try to sugarcoat the story of some deities, they too suffered deep wounds. I expanded my essay for a conference for the Ninefold Festival in 2022, where I shared about the Welsh Goddesses. And my initial essay about Arianrhod's wounds, turned into something bigger.

Although it may seem like a bad joke from the universe, while I was putting this anthology together in 2023, while still healing from past wounds (I still am), a stranger who became obsessed with me in the town where I lived began to stalk me. For months I suffered terrible harassment: he followed me on public transport, he followed me while I went to pick up my children from school, and one day he even got into my garden while my kids were playing there. It was a time of great insecurity, which opened fresh wounds and older ones. There were months of fear, a lot of anxiety, and calls to the police. Fearing for my safety, I ended up moving to another town. It wasn't easy but I had to keep going. And I had to bring these pages to life, more than ever, as an embrace to the common wounds that some of us carry.

This anthology that you are holding in your hands is a testimony of survival and resilience. Not only mine, of course, but of any women who, even deeply wounded, continues to walk hand in hand with other women, and sometimes also holding hands with some goddesses. The wounds that we share with goddesses or feminine archetypes are universal feminine wounds, which we have been carrying for thousands of years. Wounds that we also inherited from our ancestors and that unfortunately and possibly, women of future generations will also experience, while we continue to live in a patriarchal society.

As a Hierophant Priestess, I see how more and more women seek the path of the priestess as a tool of empowerment and healing. Women who seek to get closer to the divine, to the Goddess, seeking to restore their connection with the divinity, but also connecting with the possible wounds that those goddesses mirror. In a painful but beautiful and healing way, the divine wound connects with the human feminine wound, bringing closer Goddess and mortal. We've seen it with Medusa over the years, how she has become an icon of female strength and power. The Gorgon has emerged from the shadows of her own history to embrace women in their fight against patriarchal schemes. We, the women who have suffered abuse, have embraced her shadow and her wound in a desperate act to connect to her through a common wound.

But Medusa is not alone, we find these wounded deities in different cosmologies and universal folklore, and multiple references to abuse and harassment, perpetuated by Gods and men who harass goddesses and mortals alike. Jung's work is full of archetypes that he uses to try to navigate the shadows and wounds in the human psyche. Each of these goddesses has a story, has a wound that can resonate with those seeking healing. Medusa, the Irish Goddess Macha, the Welsh Arianrhod, Rhiannon, and Branwen are also examples of goddesses who are abused in the stories. Even the great Goddess Isis was beheaded by her son, although he later used magic to reverse his actions. Of course, not all wounds that we carry have to do with abuse, life itself alone can be rather traumatic and complex in many different ways. It's even harder if you are a person whose brain is wired differently, and you are neurodivergent or neurodiverse. What is normal for some, could be rather difficult for someone with sensory issues or social anxiety, or in the spectrum. Those with a deeper sensitivity are often more deeply wounded and experience a lot of suffering. There are too many wounds, there are just too many wounded Goddesses and Women out there.

This anthology is a healing journey, for those who seek aid or inspiration while healing their wounds, for those who are willing to do shadow work through the experience of the different goddesses that inhabit these pages. The idea was to go beyond re-telling their stories, you will also find some rituals and healing exercises to connect with the energy of some of the deities presented here. Some authors shared their insights about deities related to healing, like Sulis, Sekhmet, Bridgid...

This anthology is a healing gift from each of the authors who contributed to this volume. May you find the healing you need in your path. And remember, shout out for help if you need it. Look out for friends, professionals, security forces, whatever help you need. Hopefully this anthology will be of help as well.

Blessings.

Ness Bosch. 5th of July 2024.

Introduction

Isabel Alameda Jaut
(Translated by Ness Bosch)

Throughout history and in all cultures, myths have served as vehicles for transmitting not only religious beliefs but also as transmitters of social values and morals. These narratives, buried in the depths of many diverse cultures and traditions, reflect and perpetuate power dynamics within the relationships between genders in society.

From ancient times until today, it is no secret that women have faced all kinds of abuses and oppression in almost every society and culture. The abuse has been perpetuated through generations, leaving an indelible mark on the collective psyche and on the stories we tell about ourselves and our place in the world. Myths, with their ability to encapsulate the deepest truths of human experience, offer a unique window to explore these wounds and seek paths to healing and empowerment, at least that is my experience with them as a psychologist.

As Carl Gustav Jung said, "Myths are, in fact, accounts of the movements of the soul in the scenario of the external world." From Jung's analytical psychology, myths are also considered symbolic expressions of the collective unconscious. Through many of these stories, we can see how feminine archetypes, such as the mother, the lover, the healer, or the warrior, manifest and evolve over time, reflecting the experiences and conflicts of the women of that era.

In these myths, we can see, how women have faced challenges and calamities throughout history, from pain to betrayal, from darkness to death. However, We can also see how these, women and Goddesses have found strength and determination to overcome these tests and claim their power

5

and autonomy. From Greek deities to Japanese mythical figures, from the Celtic legends to Norse stories, the voices of women abused by masculine divine forces resonate throughout time. These ancestral narratives, much more than simple stories, are crucibles of experiences that invite us to understand and heal the feminine wounds that still bleed in contemporary society.

The anthology, *Divine Wounds: Finding Healing Working with Goddesses and Archetypes* seeks to explore some of these ancient stories from the perspective of modern women. More than just stories of victimisation, some of these myths or stories offer an opportunity to understand and transform profound wounds that persist in today's society. Through connection with the divine feminine and the recognition of the strength and the beauty of the feminine experience, women can find the power to heal the wounds of the past and reclaim their place in the world from empowerment and trust in themselves.

This anthology is a journey of exploration and discovery and wants to invite the reader to reflect on their own experiences and relationships with the divine feminine and the divine wounds presented in this anthology. These stories may inspire us to embrace our authenticity and reclaim our innate power as women. But also, to remind us that, despite the wounds of the past, we are indeed capable of healing and transcending that very past. We, as a collective, should work together toward a world where all women are free to live their lives with dignity, respect, and love.

Looking at the ancient Greek world, myths are populated by powerful and complex goddesses that embody different aspects of the feminine experience. Hera, the jealous wife of Zeus, symbolises the anger and resentment of women, unleashed by the works of the unfaithful masculine, opposite to Artemis who embodies the independence and strength of a woman who refuses to be subjugated. Persephone, who was 'kidnapped' by Hades and taken to the underworld, represents the experience of women who have been separated from their families by circumstances and might have lost their autonomy. And of course, I need to mention Medusa, who personifies the demonization of the feminine victim of a sexual assault.

In another of the great Greek myths, the story of Prometheus and Pandora, the figure of Pandora emerges as the very epitome of suffering. According to legend, Zeus, ruler of the Olympian gods, ordered Hephaestus to create Pandora, the very first woman, as a form of punishment to Prometheus for stealing the fire from Olympus and giving it to humanity. Pandora was gifted with a box that contained all the evil of the world. Out of curiosity, she opens the box, releasing suffering and all sorts of illnesses and adversities for humanity.

She is a woman, created from the power and the ego of the chief of the gods, and as expected, her curiosity, a mere spark of her human condition, leads her to open the box, releasing the gloom that would fall on humanity. This story is not just a distant fable; It is the painful echo of a truth that affects us as women. This myth reflects a patriarchal vision that portrays women as evil and manipulable. Women, whose mere existence is the very cause of human suffering. Throughout history, this narrative has been used to justify the oppression of women and their exclusion from roles of power in society. In ancient Greece, women were subordinates to men and were expected to fulfil domestic and child-rearing roles, while men participated in the public and military scenes.

However, when examining this myth in light of the challenges women face in the present world, we can sadly see how Pandora's story lives on reflecting on contemporary women, and the misogyny and abuse we still endure. During war times in ancient Greece, women were left to survive, alone by their own means, while men battled in war. They were faced with uncertainty and fear in their lives. But things get even worse with the arrival of Christianity. Later on, the Bible would help to promote a more negative view of women, influenced by the story of Eve in Genesis, which, as we know, portrayed her as responsible for original sin and associated her with temptation and evil. Nevertheless, by exploring the myth of Pandora from a deeper perspective, we can also find a path to healing and emancipation. As Pandora releases evil to the world, hope remains at the bottom of the box. This hope represents the possibility of a better future, where we can reclaim our place as women and work toward equality and justice, but hope also leads us to expectations and suffering sometimes, so, we need to meditate on this detail too. We need to transcend Pandora's legacy of suffering and raise our voices against oppression, and as women, begin our healing process and transformation.

Moving from Greece to Egypt, we find Nut, the goddess of the sky, and all that is above. Nut invites us to rise above, from our earthly limitations, and connect with our divine essence. We find Nut represented as a woman arched over the earth, with her body as the firmament. From an analytical perspective, the sky symbolises the transcendent, the spiritual realms, everything above, while the land represents the mundane and the materia. According to legend, Nut was the daughter of Shu, the god of air, and Tefnut, the goddess of moisture. She married Geb, the god of the earth, and together they had several children, Osiris, Isis, Seth, and Nephthys. In the myth, Nut relates to the creation of the world and the daily cycle of the sun. As the story goes, Ra, the god of the sun, decreed that Nut could not bear children on any day of the year. But Nut sought Thoth for help, and the god of wisdom, helped her to trick Ra. Thoth started by tricking the moon and gained five additional days that were not part of the original calendar and added them to the Egyptian year. During those new five days, Nut gave birth to her children: Osiris, Horus the Elder, Seth, Isis, and Nephthys. These five days became the five-day Epagomenal of the Egyptian calendar.

Ra, furious at the deception, created a new decree prohibiting Nut from giving birth on any day of the year. Nevertheless, he turned Nut's children into important gods, with crucial roles in the cosmology and the history of the Egyptians.

Nut, with her body arched over the earth, symbolises the protection and nourishment of life. Her myth reflects the importance of the sun and moon cycle in the Egyptian worldview, as well as the Connection between heaven and the land in the creation and maintenance of the world. From a humanistic perspective, Nut represents the human potential for expansion, development, and growth. Her body arched over the land suggests a loving and protective embrace, that encourages us to nurture our highest aspirations and achieve our maximum potential. In the healing process, Nut offers us a secure shelter, where we can explore our emotions deeper and work towards integration and harmony with the self.

In ancient Sumerian mythology, the myth of Inanna and Ereshkigal relates the epic journey of the goddess, Inanna, to the underworld, where her sister, Ereshkigal, reigns as the ruler of the dead. Inanna, the powerful goddess associated with love, fertility, and war, decides to undertake this journey to confront in a way, the depths of her own psyche and acquired among other things, the knowledge of the mysteries of life and death.

While descending into the dark domain of Ereshkigal, Inanna faces a series of trials and tribulations. Each door she crosses to the underworld requires her to shed a part of her divinity, until finally, she finds herself naked and vulnerable in front of her sister. Ereshkigal, instead of receiving her as a loving sister, condemns her to death. She hangs Inanna in a hook as a corpse.

While Inanna is suffering this fate in the underworld, the world above begins to fade and die. The gods, alarmed by Inanna's disappearance, send messengers to pray to Ereshkigal for her to return Inanna to life. Ereshkigal finally accepts, but demands a price: Inanna has to send someone in her place to the underworld. When she returns to the world above, Inanna discovers that her husband, Dumuzi, has been unfaithful to her, while she was away. With full determination, Inanna chooses Dumuzi as her substitute in the underworld, ensuring by doing so, her freedom.

This ancient Sumerian myth has been interpreted in many ways over the centuries. From a humanistic point of view, the myth of Inanna and Ereshkigal presents us with a story of self-awareness and personal growth. Inanna's journey to the underworld represents a process that explores the deepest and darkest aspects of the human psyche, where we face our limitations and weaknesses. The liberation of Inanna and the sacrifice of Dumuzi symbolise a personal rebirth after going through a process of confrontation and acceptance of one's own shadow. In this sense, the myth offers a powerful metaphor of the human ability to transform suffering into personal growth and renewal. Inanna emerges from the underworld with a greater understanding of herself and the world around her and she acquires the tools to live a more authentic and full life.

However, the myth of Inanna and Ereshkigal also reveals the darkness and pain that accompanies the transformation process. In today's society, many women face similar challenges in their search for self-knowledge and empowerment. From anxiety and depression to trauma and abuse, women often must face their shadows and struggles. Modern women also fight against power or forces that try to keep them in the darkness. However, just as Inanna did, we all have the potential to transform our pain into wisdom and growth. By embracing this story as a model of resilience and rebirth, today's women can find the courage to deal with their demons and claim their inner power.

Moving on to American mythology, the myth of Coatlicue offers insight into the power of feminine creativity and destruction. According to this Aztec legend, Coatlicue, the goddess of the earth and fertility, conceived Huitzilopochtli, the god of the sun and war, after being fertilised by a ball of feathers. However, her other children, the Centzon Huitznahtin, gods of the southern stars, were embarrassed by her pregnancy and decided to kill her.

This myth reflects the duality of femininity, as well as the destructive and regenerative power that resides at the heart of creation. Through the figure of Coatlicue, we see women's capacity to give life and nourish, as well as to destroy and transform. In our society, This duality is manifested in the various forms of feminine creativity and expression, as well as in the ability of women to deal with and get over adversity.

However, the myth of Coatlicue also reveals the danger that often accompanies feminine creativity. As the Centzon Huitznahtin try to kill their mother, Coatlicue fights bravely and gives birth to Huitzilopochtli in the middle of such chaos and destruction. This powerful image of the divine mother's role reflects the force and endurance of women. As well as our ability to deal with challenges and difficulties with courage and determination.

Nowadays, many women continue to fight to be recognized and valued for their creativity and talent. From art and literature to science and politics, women across the globe often face discrimination and inequality in their efforts to get their voices heard and express their ideas. By understanding the story of Coatlicue, we can look at this goddess as a symbol of feminine creativity, as a model of inspiration to continue moving forward in the search for expression and self-realisation. Through creativity and imagination, women can overcome any obstacles on our paths and we can gain the strength to create a brighter future not only for ourselves but also for future generations.

In some Celtic lands, we find myths that celebrate the magic and mysterious beauty of the natural world, personified in feminine figures such as Brigid, Rhiannon, and Morrigan. Brigid, a goddess of fire and poetry, inspires us to cultivate our creativity and passion; while Rhiannon goddess of the Moon and horses, invites us to explore the realms of the unseen and the unknown, reminding us of the importance of being open to Magic and mystery in our lives. In the Irish pantheon, Morrigan, the goddess of war and death, emerges as a figure feared and revered at the same time. Her ability to shapeshift, and foresee the destiny of men in battle, makes her a powerful female figure. Associated with crows and ravens, Morrigan personifies the duality of life and death, as well as women's ability to deal the challenges with courage and determination.

Her myth reflects the complexity of femininity and a woman's ability to adapt and transform in response to changing circumstances. Through the figure of the Morrigan, we can appreciate women's duality, as protective or destructive, as maternal and fearsome, as compassionate or ruthless. This duality manifested in the diverse shapes of femininity and in the ability of women to deal with challenges with strength and resilience.

From a humanistic psychology perspective, we see once again how myth becomes a metaphor for self-knowledge and inner growth. She pushes us to explore the deepest and darkest aspects of our psyche, recognizing our duality and complexity as human beings. By accepting and embracing our wholeness, we shall find the strength to deal with the challenges of life with courage and determination. Morrigan is a clear mirror of our inner duality, holding both light and darkness. She is a true inspiration for us to fully embrace our own authenticity and inner strength. In this sense, the stories about Morrigan offer us a powerful tool for finding meaning and purpose in our struggles and sacrifices, and for cultivating a life of growth, empowerment, and self-realisation.

We will also find in the Arthurian legends, stories of alliance and betrayal of the feminine, the history of Morgana and Guinevere (Geneva). In the legends, Morgana is portrayed as a powerful and cunning sorceress, often vilified as the evil one of the stories. However, behind her dark and mysterious facade, we find a woman whose ambition and determination challenge the social rules and the gender roles imposed by society. Morgana represents the struggle of women to claim their autonomy and power in a world dominated by men. She is often judged and condemned for her independence and her rejection of social expectations. But her story is a reminder of how important is for women to challenge the rules established and continue our path, even if we face opposition and trial from others.

On the other hand, we have Guinevere, portrayed as the wife of King Arthur, as a symbol of purity and feminine virtue. However, her relationship with Lancelot, Arthur's best friend and knight, unleashes a series of events leading Guinevere to leave Camelot. Although Guinevere is often judged and condemned for her infidelity, her story also reveals the complexity of human relationships and the internal struggles that women face in a world dominated by men.

In the icy northern lands, we also find myths that explore the wild and primordial nature of the cosmos, personified in figures like Freyja, Frigg, Hel, or Skadi. Hel, goddess of the dead, confronts us with the inevitable reality of death and the passing of time. time. Skadi, a goddess of hunting and winter, reminds us of the importance of adapting and surviving in the most hostile and challenging environments. Stories of Freyja and Frigg help us to explore the diversity of femininity and the fight for autonomy. Freyja is the goddess of love, beauty, and fertility, known for her dazzling beauty and magical skills. She is depicted as an independent and passionate figure who enjoys her freedom and refuses to give in to the wishes of men.

However, Freyja is also an ambivalent figure who embodies both the light and darkness of the female experience. She is often associated with desire and lust, which turn her into an object of desire and envy by gods and mortals alike. Her search for love and passion leads Freyja to face many challenges and dangers that test her, while Frigg, on the other hand, is the goddess of home, family, and fertility in Norse mythology, known for her devotion to her family, and her protective mother role. She is represented as a maternal and compassionate figure who looks after the well-being of her family and her community. However, her role as wife and mother, also confines her to the boundaries of the house and domestic life, limiting her autonomy.

Freyja's and Frigg's stories reflect the tensions and contradictions inherent in the feminine experience, which encompasses so much the search for love and freedom as their sacrifice. Modern women continue struggling to balance their desires and their social obligations, facing the pressure to fulfil unreal ideals of femininity and sacrifice. Learning from Freyja's passion and independence, as well as Frigg's devotion and compassion, we can forge women our own destinies and create a life that reflects our true selves.

Moving from the North to the Far East, we find myths that celebrate the beauty and harmony of the universe, personified in figures such as Inari, the goddess of rice and fertility, that reminds us of the importance of cultivating and nurturing the seeds of our hopes and dreams; so they can flourish and prosper in the world or Izanami. Through exploring the story of Goddess Amaterasu, we are faced with the duality of the light and the darkness of the feminine soul.

Amaterasu is the sun goddess in Japanese mythology, known for her radiant beauty and her kindness towards humanity. She is represented as a luminous and benevolent figure who illuminates the world with her divine light. However, Amaterasu is also a vulnerable figure who faces challenges and dangers. that threatened to eclipse her radiance. In a popular legend, Amaterasu retires to a cave as a way to complain about her brother's Susanoo betrayal, who has unleashed a series of calamities out to the world. Her absence plunges the world into darkness and chaos, making the other gods weave a plan to make her come out of her seclusion.

Izanami, the goddess of death and darkness in Japanese mythology, is associated with the underworld and the Kingdom of the Dead. It is represented as a figure mysterious and fearsome that rules over the shadows and mysteries of life and death. However, she is also a creative and fruitful force who gives birth to a multitude of gods and divine beings. The different stories about Amaterasu and Izanami offer a nuanced vision of the feminine experience, encompassing both light and darkness, life and death. Still today, women continue to face challenges and adversities that threaten to overshadow our light and steal our vitality. However, like the goddesses, we also have the power to confront the darkness and find the light inside of us.

Throughout this journey through the myths and legends of different cultures and traditions, We have explored various depths of the female experience and the wounds that women have suffered throughout history. From betrayal and abuse to the search for autonomy and empowerment, these stories are a journey of discovery and transformation of the feminine soul.

We have looked into our past to see how women have faced challenges and adversity throughout history, struggling to find their voice and mostly struggling to reclaim their power in a world that devalues and underestimates the feminine as a whole, divine, or human. But we have also seen that some of these women managed to find the strength to overcome these trials and claim their place in the world with dignity and respect.

To fully understand the impact that myths have on the female experience, It is important to analyse them from a psychological perspective. The psychology of literature can provide a conceptual framework for understanding how myths influence the way women perceive themselves and the world around them. For example, from a psychoanalytic perspective, myths can be interpreted as symbolic expressions of conflicts and unconscious desires, while from a humanist-existential perspective, myths can be seen as metaphors of the quest for self-realisation.

Using the myth of Prometheus and Pandora as an example and exploring its meaning, we can interpret Prometheus as a symbol of the dominant masculine, who seeks to control and dominate nature and women. Pandora, On the other hand, represents the passive and receptive feminine principle, which is punished for her curiosity and forbidden desires. This conflict between the masculine and feminine principles reflects in this myth the internal conflicts of women who struggle to reconcile their autonomy and their need for belonging and acceptance.

From an existential-humanist perspective, the myth of Prometheus and Pandora can be interpreted as a metaphor for the search for meaning and personal fulfillment. Pandora, open the box of evils, one faces the reality of human suffering and the fragility of existence. Without embargo, the release of hope also reveals the possibility of transformation and growth. This process of facing the darkness and finding the light within, as a fundamental part of the process of healing and empowerment of women.

By analysing each of the myths from psychology, we can see the individual and collective dimensions of the female experience. On the one hand, the myths reflect the universal conflicts and desires that all human beings face in their search for meaning and personal fulfilment. On the other hand, myths also reflect the specific social and cultural realities that influence the way women are perceived, by themselves and by the world around them. It is important to highlight that the psychological analysis of myths does not aim to reduce their meaning to mere projections of the human psyche, but rather to enrich our understanding of the complex interactions between the individual psyche and society. By recognizing and examining these interconnections, we can begin to unravel the dynamics of power and abuse that are underlined in myths, to work towards a more equal society for all.

These stories, legends, myths, and narratives provide interpretations that can sharpen our perception. The lessons they contain should build our confidence: and understanding that the path has not come to an end, but continues to guide women toward an increasingly deeper knowledge of themselves.

This anthology tries to connect us with all goddesses and archetypes that in a way we hold within. Tries to bring a message of understanding and sorority, we don't walk this journey alone. By accepting this reality, we are called to create a sisterhood, a true connection to the core of the feminine, while many of us are determined to free ourselves from burdens, stereotypes, and pre-established models to be authentic and to be who we wish to be. Recognizing our inner struggles or fights will allow us to value the challenges that other women face on their own path to empowerment. This recognition is essential to achieve success in our personal projects. So, I invite you to get to know them, understand them, explore their origins, and also love them.

And from this space that was generously offered to me, I wish to express my deep gratitude, for putting together this valuable space, trying to facilitate a tool for other women to explore, in a society that is still way too hostile towards the feminine. We need to embody the transformation that we wish to see in the world.

Macha: Healing, Betrayal, and Finding Justice

Morgan Daimler

Macha's Story is one that resonates today as much as it must have a thousand years ago in Ireland. It is a tale of a woman whose husband broke one promise which resulted in her being mocked, abused, and – in the end – getting justice through a magical curse. It is the story of a woman who trusted someone she loved, only to have his arrogance betray her to great suffering, and a woman who used magical means to gain justice when the system of justice for her culture denied her any. It is also a story of the powerless against the powerful and of a woman ensuring that the men who caused her harm came to understand her pain.

In Irish mythology there are five different appearances of a being named Macha; whether they are all the same Macha or merely share a name is uncertain. Some scholars prefer to see the five as different figures while others may see some combination of the five as overlapping. Personally, I see them as connected and as different faces of the same being; for me there is only one mythic Macha but she has many stories and each story views her slightly differently, and carries a different message.

The first Macha is the daughter of Partholon, the original settler of Ireland, although we know nothing about her and she and her people died in a plague. The second Macha was the wife of Nemed, another settler of Ireland and the eventual progenitor of both the Fir Bolg and Tuatha de Danann; this Macha is the first of her people to die in Ireland and Armagh (Ard Macha) is named for her. The third Macha is one the Tuatha de Danann and one of the three Morrigans along with her sisters, Badb and the Morrigan. This third Macha is also often considered the wife of the Tuatha De Danann king Nuada and she dies fighting at his side in the battle of Magh Tuired. The fourth Macha is a pseudo-historic queen, one of the only queens listed across Irish mythic history, and a queen who earned her crown through battle. Her father was one of three kings who shared the kingship between them, switching rule every seven years, but when Macha's father died the other two refused to acknowledge her as his rightful heir. She went to war with them and through both martial skill and cunning eventually won. Finally, we come to the fifth Macha, Macha of the Sidhe, who is our main focus here, a fairy woman who emerged into the human world inexplicably and whose life here and actions would have a profound effect on one of Ireland's greatest epic tales.

Macha's Story Retold

Once, long ago in Ireland, there was a farmer named Cruinniuc in Ulster. He was a prosperous land owner and although he was not part of the nobility, he did well enough for himself. One day a strange woman appeared and entered into his home, taking up all the duties of his wife, although he had never known her before. Nonetheless as time passed, he grew fond of the woman, whose name was Macha, and accepted her as his wife despite her unusual arrival. The two lived together happily enough as a couple and eventually Macha fell pregnant, conceiving twins with her new husband.

In the autumn of that year, when Macha was drawing near to delivering her children, the king held a harvest fair, a grand affair that would last for weeks and include feasting and games of skill, as well as trading of all sorts. Cruinniuc very much wanted to go and although Macha was reluctant, she eventually agreed, but only after she'd extracted a promise from him not to speak of her to anyone. She was a woman of the sidhe and to keep her as his wife he had to have such a geis, or sacred prohibition, placed on him; if he broke his word then she would have no choice but to leave him. However, while he was at the fair he heard the king's poet praising the speed of the royal horses who had won all the day's races and, having already had enough ale to loosen his tongue and limit his common sense, Cruinniuc loudly boasted that his wife could run faster than any horses, including the king's best. Furious the king demanded that Cruinniuc's wife be brought to the assembly to show everyone how foolish his words were; Cruinniuc was seized by the king's warriors and a messenger was sent to bring Macha. When the messenger arrived and explained that she needed to come to the fair because of her husband's boasting she refused, saying that she was in labour. The messenger then explained that if she did not go her husband would be executed. Lamenting his foolish words, she followed the man to the fairgrounds.

Once there the king declared she must race against the horses herself or her husband would be killed. She asked for a delay so that she could give birth first, but he denied her request, telling the warriors to pull their swords and kill Cruinniuc. Desperate, she turned to the gathered crowd and begged them to grant her time to have her child before running, reminding them that they were all born of a mother. But the crowd, like the king, was not moved by her pleas; she saw neither pity not mercy in their eyes, and her heart hardened with anger. She warned them that a curse would fall upon them for what they were doing but still they made her go to the starting line, next to the chariot with the king's horses.

As soon as the race began, she flew forward, faster than the wind, easily running the length of the track and crossing the finish line long before the horses. She fell down after winning and there on the race track she gave birth to her children, a daughter named Honour and a son named Truth. When she gave birth, she cried out and the entire crowd was seized with the feelings of a woman in childbed. She was holding both babies when the king's horses finally crossed the finish line next to her.

She stood and surveyed the crowd which had fallen silent except for some small moaning and crying. She held her children closer and said in a loud carrying voice, "From this moment until nine generations are spent, whenever the people of this province are in the greatest hour of need you will be consumed by the pain and the weakness of a woman giving birth. For five days and four nights you will be helpless and powerless to defend yourselves, just as you have made me feel today." With those final words she disappeared back into the Otherworld from whence she'd come, taking her twins with her. From that day the place bore the name Emain Macha, Twins of Macha, in remembrance of her, and from that day for nine following generations the men if Ulster were rendered helpless for five days and four nights when they were most in need, as Macha's curse effected both the people present when she raced and their descendants. This curse was pivotal to the events of the epic Táin Bó Cúailgne, because it was for this reason that the men of Ulster were helpless when Connacht attacked, leaving only the half-Tuatha De Danann hero, Cu Chulainn, able to defend them.

Message of the Tale

The story of Macha is the story of a woman who is betrayed by the man she loves, because he cannot resist bragging. Whether he did it out of insecurity or genuine pride in his wife's speed, whether he did it to try to impress the king or because he spoke without thinking, the result was the same. He broke the single promise she had asked him to make; he betrayed her trust. And that betrayal created a domino effect of consequences that she had to suffer through: being dragged in front of a crowd despite being in labour, being forced to race against horses, and having to give birth before an entire hostile crowd. In the culture of the time, it was considered inappropriate for men to see a woman in labour or giving birth, it was a private situation, and so having to do so publicly would have been shameful for Macha,

21

her personal situation put on display for strangers. She begged them for a delay – not to get out of racing completely nor to be allowed to leave entirely, but only for a delay so that she could give birth first. It was a small act of mercy amid the cruelty of the situation but even that wasn't granted. She had no choice but to push through both her physical pain and the emotional pain of the situation.

At different points in our lives we are all like Macha the fairy woman, we are all forced to push through impossible situations. While her story is sad it is also a lesson in perseverance and speaks to the power of overcoming insurmountable obstacles through sheer stubbornness. Macha doesn't give up despite the situation and her pain, and she wins in the ends. There is inspiration in that, and in the knowledge that ultimately it is the bullies who suffer the most because of their own actions. That ending doesn't justify or even ease the pain that she goes through but it offers hope to all of us, I think, because it shows us that sometimes the victim does ultimately come out better than the people who have abused her. She is betrayed, publicly mocked and shamed, made to suffer physically, yet in the end she is the one who is victorious, both in winning the race and in cursing the crowd. Macha teaches us the power of perseverance against any odds.

Macha's story is also one of honourable actions in dishonourable circumstances. Her husband breaks his promise, after being warned of the consequences, and yet she doesn't abandon him to execution. She could very easily have simply left when the messenger came to tell her that she was being summoned to the fairgrounds. She could have refused to race when the crowd didn't offer her any mercy as she begged. She could have let her husband die as a consequence of his own hasty words. But she didn't do any of that, she stayed and despite the pain she raced, and she won. She only left after she had won and her husband's life was saved. Despite everything she chose to remain honourable and to act honourably, and the names she chose for her son and daughter reflect that significance of that choice. The world around her and the person she loved showed her nothing but dishonourable behaviour but she held true to her own honour. As tempting as it often is to sink to the other person's level when we are faced with grossly unfair situations in our own lives, Macha speaks of the power of staying true to ourselves and valuing our own integrity over retaliation. She teaches us to value ourselves. No matter the circumstances.

Justice is something that should be clearcut but rarely is, and it is something that should be available to everyone equally but rarely is. The shape of justice can be nebulous and ephemeral and often hard to grasp. Macha the fairy woman is a stranger to the people around her, except her husband, a person who has no extended family ties or connections to the people around her. She is a foreigner and a woman, both things that make justice harder for her to get. The king denies her, the crowd denies her, and her husband – the one person who could legally defend her – remains silent. Instead of justice she receives injustice, forced to race when she should be granted mercy. Yet in the end she is the arbiter of justice, she is the one who deals out the ultimate retribution for the actions of those who have caused her this harm – through the vehicle of magic she curses them all to experience what she has experienced, what other women birthing children experience – she literally makes them all equal to her in her moment of greatest suffering, and inflicts it on them, as it was inflicted on her, in their moment of greatest need. She isn't punishing them to make them suffer but to teach them the value of mercy. The men she cursed couldn't imagine the physical or mental pain she had to push through so she made them experience for themselves what she experienced.

Generational curses are rare but powerful things, energy which attaches to a family or group and lingers until it has worked itself out. In discussing Macha the fairy woman and justice it may seem odd that she didn't just curse the crowd in front of her but cursed the people for nine generations, and that may seem unfair – why after all would people who hadn't even been born yet, whose grandparents hadn't even been born yet, deserve to suffer for the actions of their ancestors? But the truth is that we all carry forward with us the actions of those who have gone before, good or bad, and we all bear the burden of those actions. In a way Macha's curse is an example of this. In another way it is an example of what it can take to change ingrained ideas and behaviour. Perhaps cursing nine generations was something that she saw as necessary to ensure that those future generations didn't repeat the mistakes of the older one, to help them all to understand the value of mercy and justice until it was ingrained in them to be better people. Perhaps sometimes true justice isn't only looking at ways to restore the balance of a current situation and repay a person who has been wronged but also looking at ways to prevent the same situation from repeating, if possible. Perhaps cursing nine generations was the best way for Macha to ensure that true justice was done and that justice became part of the fabric of that community.

Macha's curse is about empathy, about teaching people who lack the ability to understand another person's pain by letting them experience it for themselves. It is an aggressive lesson, a teaching method that doesn't allow any room to rationalise away the other person's pain because they are made to feel it in full in their own bodies. This may seem harsh but if we really look at the story, we see that it was the only option in the end. Macha, a woman of the Otherworld, was always powerful enough to stop what was happening to her but all of the other people, all of the other women, put in similar terrible situations could not. So, she allowed the situation to play out, she allowed herself to be ill-treated, she raced, and laboured, and birthed in public, because it allowed her to protect not herself but every other helpless person. Everyone else who was denied mercy, who's cries went unheard and whose pleas were ignored. Her curse wasn't for herself, in the end, but for all the helpless people across that group and across the ensuing nine generations who might be shielded instead of harmed. It was a justice that looked to the future and to the greatest weapon against bullying – empathy.

Personal Takeaway

The story of Macha the fairy woman has always been one of my favourites and also one that spoke loudly to me. Growing up I dealt with several difficult situations, including abuse and bullying, and it was easy to feel hopeless and to feel like the people who were supposed to help me had chosen instead to make the situation worse. Macha's race, for me, became a metaphor for the struggle of daily life and the need to keep fighting – to keep racing – no matter how difficult the situation was. Macha suffered, and in the end, she overcame that suffering and while it cost her it also allowed her to find justice and to teach others the value of mercy.

Her lessons also came back to me after the birth of my youngest child, when a rare postpartum complication nearly killed me. It was a terrible time and a terrible experience but it was one in which I needed the comfort of a story and of goddess who understood suffering and pushing through physical pain. I needed to be able to look to a story, to Macha's story, for hope and a reminder that sometimes all we can do is keep putting one foot in front of the other until we find the finish line. Perhaps that seems like a strange lesson to take away from her story but it kept me going in a time when I wasn't sure I could survive.

I encourage people to look to Macha during pregnancy and birth because I think that her story also works on a metaphoric level for those things. In a different way than the other lessons we can take from her tale we can also find a story of healing and of endurance during the messy, unpleasant physical processes of creating and birthing a child. What we are going through she has gone through, not as a goddess but as the willing wife of a mortal man, someone who chose to live in the human world and who gave birth under the most difficult conditions imaginable, after running a race with her husband's life on the line. She understands that process and the pain we might experience during it better than many other deities. Just as she taught the men of Ulster to empathize with her pain, she can empathize with ours.

Macha is a powerful figure, no matter what guise we are looking at, but Macha the fairy Woman can be especially so. She is a good goddess to connect to if you are dealing with personal betrayals, particularly by loved ones, if you are dealing with bullying or the consequences of peer pressure, or if you are experiencing a difficult pregnancy or birth. Her energy speaks to overcoming both mental and physical pain during times of crisis, and she is a figure which can be leaned on for that strength. She also helps us better understand the value of mercy and the power of reparative justice over forgiveness.

Macha the Fairy Woman

I loved a mortal man once
To my grief, I loved him
Even now, after all the pain
And blood and tears
Even now I still love him
Because love isn't a simple
Thing that can be willed away
I love him. I loved him.
And he betrayed me.

I made him promise, before
He left for the king's fair
I made him promise not to
Speak a word of me

His silence was supposed to
Be my shield, my protection
But he drank too much and
Grew too bold. He spoke.
He broke his word.

The king's men came for me
To make me prove his words
To prove I could run faster
Than the king's horses
I told them that my womb was
Heavy with twins, restless
And ready to be born now
They told me that I would
Run or he would die.

I begged them, begged for time
Begged to wait, begged for mercy
Their hearts had none
I ran through the suffering because
I had no choice but to be strong
My body wracked with pain
My feet swifter than the wind
I ran through the agony and blood
I ran through the heartache
I ran for his life

So swift was I, so fast on
the course, the horses were
left far behind
I won, and I fell, and my
Children were born in the dirt
Of the racetrack as I wept
I won, but the cost was high

I was a woman of Fairy
To Fairy I returned

Before I left this mortal world
I cursed the men who had cost
Me my life, my love
I cursed the crowd that watched
On, unmoved, as I begged them
For any delay, any reprieve
I cursed them to feel my pain
To suffer as I had suffered
When the hour of their greatest
Need was upon them

Because I won
But it cost me everything.

Connecting to Macha the Fairy Woman

The easiest and first way that I recommend for people to start connecting to this aspect of Macha is by reading her story, which can be found in the Dindshenchas, or place name stories, of Irish mythology, specifically those around Emain Macha, and in the Ulster Cycle tales under the name 'Noínden Ulad' or the Debility of the Ulsterman. These stories can be found free online or in various books, either as translations of the original or as retellings. Understanding her story and its variations helps to gain a wider understanding of who she is and to start building a rapport with her. You can meditate on the stories after reading them and see what aspects speak the loudest to you and which ones make you uncomfortable. It's alright if some parts of her story make you feel uneasy or unhappy but it's important to try to sort out why those feelings are there. Macha can be a wonderful guide to reclaiming our own personal power but often that can only occur by working through the hidden things that are holding us back. Exploring the good and bad of her tale is a start.

Another good way to begin connecting to Macha is to create a small alter or shrine for her. This can be as simple or as complex as you like, but here are some suggestions for things you can incorporate. Macha is sometimes called 'the sun of womanhood' so incorporating solar colours like yellow, red, and orange might work well, as would gold. Because of her race with the king's horses and because one of Cu Chulainn's horses was named 'the grey of Macha' she is often associated with or connected to horses so having some sort of horse images or statues or items on your altar can also be a good idea; however, I advise against having anything that might have been created from a horse through violent means. If you can't be a hundred percent certain that something was sourced ethically, don't use it. Another thing that I personally use is statues or images of goddesses who are pregnant or who have twin infants. It can be extremely difficult to find these images of Macha specifically so I will repurpose others by blessing them in Macha's name and consecrating them to her. Beyond that it can be a very individual process to create an altar or a shrine and you should choose things that speak to you and which make you feel closer to Macha in this particular guise, as the fairy woman rather than the war goddess.

Macha the fairy woman, as a face of the Irish goddess Macha, is a powerful transformative force. She is an example to us of what we can accomplish if we persevere, a reminder that life can be unfair and even cruel – that the people we love may betray us and the authority figures meant to protect us may hurt us instead – and she is an example of the way we can heal and reclaim our own power by remaining honourable and in seeking justice. She speaks to women, to people struggling through pregnancy, but she also speaks more generally to the helpless and those treated unfairly. We can look at her story, the story of a powerful being who was treated badly by the humans around her, and see that the shape of justice isn't always retribution, but sometimes can be healing through pain. And we can look to her and see the power of survival through leaving a bad situation to find safety elsewhere.

Finding Healing Working
with Welsh Goddesses

Ness Bosch

This is a personal exploration of the magical ladies or Welsh Goddesses that appear in the *Mabinogion*. I say ladies because in reality there is no mention that they are Goddesses, but their magic is mentioned, which could lead us to understand that they are Goddesses who survived in oral Welsh culture, suffering metamorphosis in their stories until finally, these stories are compiled in writing in the *Mabinogion*. In this exploration, we will move away from the sugary or sometimes sexualized version that has been given of some of these Goddesses. This is an exploration in brief of the shadow in the stories of these magical women because unfortunately, part of that shadow is still very relevant. I followed the order of appearance of female characters in the *Mabinogion*, I would have to start with The Lady of Annwfn, but I'm going to start my essay with Arianrhod since I have come closer to her this year.

Arianrhod, a Welsh Goddess that is related to magic, the sea, and the stars, is also associated with reincarnation, destiny in the form of fate, shapeshifting, and the Moon. When analysing her story from a feminist perspective, we are faced with disheartening myth for many reasons. With those points in mind, let us review the myth of Arianrhod, according to the story of Math found in the *Mabinogion*, also known as the Fourth Branch of the *Mabinogion*.

Arianrhod, daughter of Don (the Welsh equivalent of the Irish Goddess Danu) was together with her brothers, Gwydion and Gilfaethwy, a member of the court of King Math, who appears as her Uncle in various writings. This was no ordinary man, Math, son of Mathonwy, possessed magical powers and suffered from a taboo or curse. Unless he were at war, a virgin maiden had to hold his feet in her lap or he would die. For this reason, Math barely left his kingdom and had given the virgin, Goewin, the responsibility of holding his feet.

The story goes that one of the brothers of Arianrhod, Gilfaethwy, had a fervent carnal desire towards Goewin. To help him his brother, Gwydion, contrived to create a conflict with the south with the sole intention that Math would abandon his kingdom and Goewin. Unfortunately, the trick works and while Math is in the south, the two brothers return to the castle and rape Goewin. Upon Math's return, she confesses that she has been outraged by the brothers so that she will no longer be able to hold the monarch's feet to prevent his death. Goewin has lost her status and purity. She is no longer good enough to serve him.

To repair the affront Math marries her and decides to punish the brothers. Gwydion and Gilfaethwy are forced to return to court to face the King's justice for their affront to Goewin. Math magically turns them into animals and for three years, they would change into animal forms. Not only that, they were cursed to conceive a child between them every year. These children were then taken by Math, who gave them human form and baptized them.

After those three years of punishment, Math brings the brothers back to court and he forgives them. Gwydion tries to make amends by offering Math his sister, Arianrhod, as a virgin, a deal the king accepts if she passes a virginity test. According to the myth Arianrhod accepts this test. Math makes Arianrhod jump over his "magic wand", whereupon, as if by magic, the former maiden gives birth to a boy, but something else comes from her after that boy. That thing, whatever it was, will later become a baby boy too.

Math takes the boy with curly blond hair and baptises him with the name of Dylan and he makes his way to the sea where he undergoes a magical transformation and takes on the nature of the sea. The 'small something' is hidden by Arianrhod's brother, Gwydion, and eventually matures into an infant. Gwydion takes him to the city and gives the boy to a woman to nurse at her breast. Like his brother, this child is magical and the story tells how he grew at a speed above human and that after a few years, he made a place for himself in the court, next to his uncle. As the years go by, Gwydion pays a visit to his sister Arianrhod and takes the unnamed child with him. Upon revelation of the true identity of the creature to his mother, she goes into a rage, feeling once again humiliated. When her brother declares the boy has no name, obviously hoping for his mother to give him one, she refuses. Furious and hurt, she puts a taboo or fate on the child that he would never get a name if it wasn't from her hand.

Gwydion once again uses tricks and cunning and, disguised as shoemakers, they return to visit the castle to trick his sister. She unknowingly gives the child, her son, the name of Lleu Skillful-Hand. Her brother triumphantly reveals the identity of both and humiliated Arianrhod once again puts a taboo on her son, that he would never get weapons until she would arm him herself.

Gwydion and the boy retire for a few years from the public scene while Lleu becomes a young man. Once again, his uncle plans a trick so that his sister will give the young man arms. They get on horseback and head to his sister's castle, where once again, hiding their identity, they are received with honor. At dawn, by magic, he simulates an attack on the castle and Lady Arianrhod seeks for him, requesting his help and protection, offering them both arms. Triumphant once more, he reveals his identity and his sister once again imposes a taboo on her child, this time that he could not get a wife, from any race in the world.

Once again, her brother challenges her, accusing Arianrhod of being a bad woman and mother and declares that the boy will get his wife despite the curse. But achieving this was not going to be easy, as she specified very clearly that the woman could not be of this world.

Gwydion decides to take the boy, who was by now a mature and handsome young man, to the court of Math for help. Once there, Gwydion complains against Arianrhod, trying to obtain favors for his nephew and we assume that Math takes pity on the young man. Making use of their magical powers, Math and Gwydion create the most beautiful maiden ever seen at court, Blodeuedd, from flowers. The couple marry and retire to live on lands that are given to them by Math.

The next part of the story continues no longer including mention of Arianrhod (who spends her days in Caer Arianrhod) but focusing on the bride and groom.

As the story goes, Blodeuedd falls in love with Gronw Pebr. Together they conspire to kill Lleu but he is brought back to life by his uncle Gwydion. As punishment, Blodeuedd is transformed into an Owl, cursed to fly in the shadows and be hated by all, and her lover is killed by Lleu's hand.

And this is the end of the Fourth Branch of the *Mabinogion*.

Not only from the beginning, the story presents us with Math as a man who hides behind the feminine power of the virgin maiden, where Goewin represents the Kore. After being raped by Arianrhod's brothers, she apologizes to Math, even trying to justify that she resisted and that her servants heard her scream, still feeling guilty about it. The person who transmits the story makes clear that Goewin emotionally detaches from her trauma and starts feeling guilty for not being able to serve her lord. We might consider the possible psychological sequels, and physical injuries of a multiple rape.

The brothers spend three years of punishment, and then to placate Math and seek his forgiveness, Gwydion offers their sister to be his maiden. Arianrhod is used as a currency, but Math goes further and organises a virginity test, for which she has to step over on his magic wand is too explicit to ignore the sexual connotations of it. Especially when the result of that test is a pregnancy. Could Math have sexually taken Arianrhod to prove that she was a virgin? The story says that he asks her to step and she does it voluntarily, perhaps out of honor and to prove her truth. But we know that sexual coercion is a reality, he is the monarch and she is pushed to comply with the test by her brother.

Either way she goes through the test. Of course, what happens next is very magical, but we must not forget that Math is a magician and that Arianrhod also has magical and divine blood. So that spontaneous birth happens because during the test Math makes Arianrhod pregnant. Of course, she gets angry and embarrassed. Her brothers have used her, offering her to Math as if she were a sheep. He has publicly put her to the test, after which she is no longer a virgin and on top of that he has made her pregnant. She gives birth to a child, but another child appears magically, this is a reflection of Arianrhod's world, which lies between magic and the world of men.

I could tell you right now, in the year 2022 the story of a girl who is abused and ashamed. I could tell you that her children are taken from her at birth, in the midst of a highly traumatic situation, after which she retires to a safe place. If I tell you that after a few years, one of her perpetrators approaches her with one of her children, demanding her to recognize him. Would you be surprised by Arianrhod's reaction? She would not be the first woman to reject a child who was fruit of a humiliation or rape. Because that child is living proof of her pain and shame.

When in the myth, Arianrhod appears to be punishing the boy with a fate, she might be actually trying to punish the masculine gender in general for her pain and specifically her brother for coming to open her wounds and expose her once again to shame. She is not a loving mother, we cannot expect her to be as she is emotionally dissociated from the child. She took refuge in her castle and has tried to live her life as if nothing had happened. The story even mentions that Gwydion mocks her for no longer being a maiden, reminding her that she has already been a mother and given birth.

Arianrhod imposes a fate on her son, first so he cannot get a name, then that he cannot be armed, and finally that he cannot take a wife. The first curse, the denial of an identity, can perfectly be linked to the male ego. The destruction of the ego through the denial of the personality, in this case identified in the name. Arianrhod denies her son arms in the second curse, she would clearly be denying him power: that masculine power, used-abused by many men and for which she herself has suffered. In the third curse she denies Lleu the possibility of mating with a woman. Perhaps with the intention of not giving him the possibility that as a man, he could abuse or harm a female. She is trying to curse men, really. I personally think so.

It is true that it is a sad situation, but she is not really being given the possibility of connecting with her son. Nobody here is fostering a positive or real rapprochement between a mother and a child. What we are witnessing is once again an abuse of the patriarchy towards Arianrhod, in which Gwydion imposes his will and finds himself offended by his sister's lack of cooperation.

Gwydion, his ego insulted by Arianrhod's attitude, heads to Math's court with Lleu. In this part of the story, we once again witness another outburst of male ego. Arianrhod is judged again and both men see themselves with the right to change the destiny that she has imposed on her son. Arianrhod is condemned to oblivion after this episode and her refusal to help with her brother is in fact the trigger for the appearance of another of the Goddesses in the *Mabinogion*.

In the story of Arianrhod we clearly meet abuse. She is a victim of coercive control by her brothers and I think we won't be too wrong to label Math abusive and a narcissist, both because of his behavior using Goewin, because of her connection with the land. Sexual abuse is implicit in her story even beyond what we read, as there are people who believe that Goewin's character is an attempt to soften Arianrhod's own story, and that Arianrhod would have been the maiden who is raped by her brothers and originally, she held Math's feet. Only that this incestuous story had been censored at some point.

Following the thread of the story of Arianrhod I would like to continue with an introduction to Blodeuedd.

She is a woman magically created by and for a man. Gwydion and Maths combine their powers and from their ego, create a woman as an accessory and without apparent will, at least initially, since the text says that Blodeuedd and Lleu lie together during the celebrations, since Blodeuedd is made for and given to Lleu. We can go further on a psychological analysis, because Blodeuedd has not even had time to assume her own existence and finds herself in the arms and possession of a stranger.

Blodeuedd doesn't seem to have her own will or feelings of her own to start with, later she falls in love with another, Gronw Pebyr. She falls in love and gives herself sexually to him. The story tells how the lovers decide that Lleu's death is the only way for Blodeuedd to be freed from that union.

Now, I would like to analyse the character of Gronw Pebyr. The story makes their meeting somewhat romantic but we don't really know his real intentions and why he seduces Blodeuedd. The lovers could have escaped to love elsewhere without resorting to murder. But I will venture to say that Blodeuedd is not only beautiful, her husband has a castle and lands that were given to him by Math. If Gronw Pebyr had only wanted her, wouldn't running away together have been a good option? Gronw Pebyr's intentions may not have been as romantic as they are presented in the story. But he convinces Blodeuedd, or so we can interpret, that he loves her and that the only way to be together is that he has to figure out how to kill Lleu, which they end up doing after which Gronw takes possession of Lleu's assets. What we have before us in this part of the story could very well be a predator hunting his prey, Blodeuedd, by and for his benefit. By magical arts, Lleu is resurrected by Gwydion. Once recovered, Lleu demands justice and Gwydion grants it, starting by punishing Blodeuedd.

We clearly find different kinds of abuse in Blodeuwedd's story. She is created without apparent will to make her husband happy, but she is manipulated by a man to kill her husband, for his territory and position and she follows him. But we don't have to assume that she's fully aware of what they're doing. We have to remember that she's not human, she doesn't have human consciousness.

Another main character of the *Mabinogion* is Rhiannon and also a popular Celtic Goddess. Rhiannon is related to horses, as a diffusion/evolution of the continental Goddess Epona in Britain, as would be the Goddess Macha in Ireland. She is a Sovereign Goddess and she represents the land as we clearly see in her story, but her sovereignty does not save her from having a bad time. Her tale is quite tragic too.

In short, Rhiannon was going to be forced to marry someone and in order to escape her fate she goes looking for Pwyll. Rhiannon explains how she is going to be married to another but that in reality she wants him and hopes that he will help her escape that arranged marriage. And so Pwyll does and after humiliating her suitor, Gwawl, they get married.

Rhiannon will give birth to a child who magically disappears after birth. The baby's disappearance comes as such a shock that the nannies in charge of the baby, in order not to be punished, devise a plan to blame Rhiannon, which they do. The queen is accused of having murdered her own son and gets punished by

Pwyll to carrying people like a horse on her back and telling the story of her misfortune.

Meanwhile, her baby ends up in the house of some noble people, also in a magical way. They raise him and over the years they discover that the child is the son of the king and queen and return him to court, thus freeing Rhiannon from her punishment and her guilt.

But Rhiannon's story continues in the *Mabinogion*. Years have gone by and she is older and now a widow. Without her knowledge, her son, Pryderi, gives her in marriage to a friend of his, Manawydan, although later she accepts. During the story her kingdom magically disappears when she ends up imprisoned trying to help her son. At the end her kingdom appears once more and it is revealed that she had been enchanted in revenge for her rejection and mocking of Gwawl earlier in the story. Clearly, she, as a representation of the land, is the one that grants power and control of the territory, but that does not save her from being unjustly accused and punished by her husband in a humiliating way. Her beauty and her sovereignty are somehow a curse in which they bring her misfortunes. But not only to her, when Rhiannon is trapped, her kingdom disappears for that very reason, because she is the land.

Another of the magical women with some relevance in the *Mabinogion* is Branwen.

She is a princess, daughter of Llyr, sister of Bendigeidfran, the Giant King. As with other women of the *Mabinogion*, Branwen is used as a bargaining chip, given in marriage to the King of Ireland, Matholwch, who crosses the sea to ask the king for her hand and thus unify the two islands.

The text makes it clear that it is a political decision and does not mention whether Branwen agrees or not, but once again we see the role of the noble woman, sovereign with a strong connection to the land, subject to the decisions and politics of men. During the celebrations, Efnisien, half-brother of the King and Branwen, learns of his sister's marriage and, not agreeing with the union, proceeds to take revenge on the King of Ireland by mutilating his horses. After this action, of course, there is trouble and Bendigeidfran tries to put a remedy to it by offering gifts to Matholwch, who takes them and leaves the next day with Branwen.

Once in Ireland, she lives peacefully and happily and she gives birth to a son. People love her and she is treated with respect, until the story of what happened to Matholwch's horses in Anglesey becomes public. At that time the King's brothers request that he punishes Branwen or risk losing his crown and kingdom. Faced with such a threat, Matholwch snatches Branwen from her position as Queen and sends her to the kitchens where, apart from working as a commoner, she is physically punished every day.

A bird, a starling, will help Branwen carry a message to her brother the King. Bendigeidfran and Efnisien will cross the sea with their men. Efnisien takes the opportunity to kill Branwen's son by throwing him into the fire in revenge and the Irish lose the battle. Only seven Welsh soldiers return to Anglesey and poor Branwen heartbroken with grief, for her son, her brothers and both kingdoms.

Branwen is not only a victim of the control of the men in the story, they humiliate and physically abuse her, as part of a punishment that is not hers to receive. In addition, her own brother murders her son, a clear example of sexist violence.

There are other women who appear briefly in the four branches of the *Mabinogion*, at the beginning I mentioned The Lady of Annwfn, who is given by her husband to another man to sleep with her for a whole year and then is refused by that very man, we also saw Goewin in the story of Arianrhod, who is raped by Arianrhod's brothers.

Now that we know the history of the Welsh Goddesses and their scars. How many of those wounds are familiar to you? We may not be living in that age anymore, but there is still abuse, it happens to our friends, our neighbours, it has happened to us. The #MeToo movement made it very clear, that abuse lives on. Data on coercive control, narcissistic abuse has exploded in recent years, perhaps because not so long ago this type of abuse was not recognized as such. It is a silent but highly destructive abuse.

None of the women mentioned escapes the control of a man, none. It doesn't matter how sovereign, how beautiful, how intelligent they may be. Because Rhiannon wasn't an idiot, neither was Arianrhod or Branwen. They were ladies of high birth, with royal and magical blood in some cases. They were powerful women. And yet they all suffered abuse. But let's not forget something, narcissists like women with power, to feed on them. Of course, the abuse they inflict is not enough, we see very clearly in Arianrhod's story, how the narcissists after abusing her, judge her publicly and strive to stain her name with shame.

The narcissist is not content with abusing you, he will destroy every connection you have with the rest of the world, they make up stories to cover up their actions, to justify themselves. After mentally abusing you, the next thing is to try to eliminate the supports that you could get from friends and people around you and for this it is important to stain your public image. Just as it happens to Arianrhod that she finds herself condemned to a solitary exile in her castle, tainted by the actions of others and her own, born from manipulation and trauma.

Walking together with the Welsh Goddesses, in recognition of common wounds, we can begin to walk towards our healing, because recognition is an important part of this process and they are a great mirror for every woman who has suffered some type of abuse. Something that I realized is that these Goddesses are somehow quite accessible. Perhaps because they are not implicitly called Goddesses, it brings them closer to us, which facilitates being able to establish a devotional relationship or communicating with them.

Arianrhod, Lady of Sorrow

Arianrhod,
you forget your sorrow
looking at the sea,
hidden between
cold and wet walls.
Your shame is not yours
It is not!
Shame on those
who dared to take advantage
of your innocence and beauty.
Not all the magic of Don
was able to protect her daughter
from her own blood.
Abuse, lies and tricks!
Damn men!
Damn Gilfaethwy!
Damn Gwydion and
Damn the Great Math!
Damn them all
and their men's games!
What didn't they take from you?
beautiful Arianrhod.
What did they leave you?
shame and sorrow,
loneliness and stone
sea songs,
salt and storm,
stars…

From the shadows,
the silence and
your freedom.
Ness Bosch. 2022.

How to Create an Altar to Honour Arianrhod

Arianrhod relates closely to the moon and stars, also to the seashore, so you can use things you would find while walking along the beach to connect with her. She is also connected with the Corona Borealis, with the silver wheel and weaving. When I think about her the colours blue, in its darker shades, even purple comes to me. Also, silver and white, the colours of the Moon. As she relates to the stars, I also see how sparkly silvery things could be used to place on her altar. Silver jewellery to wear to connect with her during devotional work. She is said to shapeshift into an owl, so anything to do with owls will work too. I like working with crystals and I have used them for years. When I think about crystals and Arianrhod, I think, of course, of Silver, Pyrite, Galena, Hematite, Antimonite (but mind as it is toxic, so I use it for protective magic working with Arianrhod), Blue or Purple Labradorite (Hypersthene), Blue Moonstone, Preseli Stone, Dumortierite, Sodalite, Blue Kyanite, Sapphire or corindon, Larvikite, Magnesite, natural white Howlite, fossils like Ammonite found on the coast.

To create a basic Altar to honour Arianrhod you could use a deep blue fabric. silver or glass candleholders. Some seashells or coral, blue or white if so. Silver colour trinkets to place offerings. You could offer her white or blue flowers or fruits, like blueberries, grapes or plumbs. There are plants that are kind of silvery-metallic in colour you could offer her. You could also knit or crochet something for her. Silver or silver colour coins are also good to be placed on the altar. You can also include the symbol of the owl in any form and any of the crystals I listed above.

Ritual to Seal a Fate with the Help of the Welsh Goddesses

For this ritual we will need:

Something Blue related to the Sea or dark blue flowers, a dark blue stone or a Silver Coin.

Something Yellow, Yellow Flowers or an owl-shaped charm.

Something White, Flowers or White Marble or a white feather, a charm related to horses or horsehair.

Something Green, Heliotrope Stone or Cauldron or Goblet.

Consecrated water.

A floating candle.

A veil.

A mirror.

Primrose oil.

Blue ink.

Flowers and food for offerings.

A large bowl or cauldron.

Floral water to cleanse the space.

With this ritual we are going to cast a fate for someone who has hurt us, with the help of four Welsh Goddesses. Arianrhod, Rhiannon, Branwen and Blodeuwedd. This is also a protection ritual.

We'll have to purify space to begin with. To honor Arianrhod, we can wear something blue.

We will prepare our offerings for the Goddesses and prepare our bowl with water. We will put on the veil at this time before continuing.

We will take the silver coin or the element related to Arianrhod and holding it in our hand we will invoke the Goddess. Then we will throw the coin into the water. Next, we will take the owl-shaped charm and proceed to invoke Blodeuwedd. And we will deliver the Charm to the water.

We will do the same with the white feather and after invoking Rhiannon we will deliver the feather to the water. Finally, we will take the Heliotrope stone to invoke Branwen and we will deliver it to the water as well.

After making the invocations, we will deposit the primrose oil in the water. Not too much. We will light the floating candle.

And after a minute of connection with the story of Arianrhod and the other Goddesses, we will take the blue ink and deposit the ink in the water in circles. Next take a few minutes to find the oracle or destiny (the words) in the water and take the silver hand mirror in your hand reflecting it out. Connect with the energy of Arianrhod and with your own story and let destiny flow from your lips, for the person who inflicted suffering on you as you move with the mirror in a circle around you, all energy, all action, all sick intention that has been projected onto you by that person or others on their behalf.

If there is a Full Moon, keep directing the energy while you pronounce the destiny, and turn the mirror towards the light of the Moon to end the ritual, capturing its light, using the Moon as a mirror, so that these energies are returned magnified to their origin and at the same time send the destiny to your recipient.

Thank the Moon and The Goddesses for their help and deposit the mirror at the altar with the reflecting side facing down.

Now you can remove your veil. Ritual is finished.

Healing with Lake Ladies
and Well Maiden

Annwyn Avalon

Within Celtic mythology, we find numerous deities, spirits, and beings that are connected with water. Two of these groups of watery beings are the Lake Ladies and Well Maiden. Both are subaquatic spirits who sometimes appear singularly but often times in groups or clusters. They also both belong to bodies of fresh water and are generous beautiful spirits.

We have several stories in Celtic Mythology and Folklore that tell us of Lake Ladies. Perhaps you have heard of Nimue and Vivian from the legends of King Arthur and his knights. There are, however, legends that are much older than those of Nimue and Vivian. In the *Mabinogi*, which contains ancient stories of Wales we find a story called the Lady of the Lake. In this story we are introduced to a young shepherd that is resting beside a lake in Brecon Beacons called Llyn Y Fan Fach.

As he is resting, a beautiful maiden emerges from the water and asks him to share his bread. He is struck by her beauty and shares the bread with her. She tells him it is not to her liking; it is too hard. She then asked him to return the next day with a loaf of bread that was softer. The shepherd does just that and returns the next day with another loaf of bread to share with her. This time she tells him that the bread is too soft and asks if he could return a third time with bread that was neither too soft nor too hard. He returns the following day with a third loaf of bread. She is so pleased that she agrees to marry him on one condition. That he may not strike her three times. He agrees and they marry. She brings with her a large dowry of cows that followed her out of the lake.

They lived together happily for some time and had three sons. Time passes but the shepherd can't keep his promises. One day they were invited to a wedding. As they were getting ready to leave the lake lady remembered she had forgotten her gloves in the house. She agrees to finish getting the horses ready if her husband runs into the house to get her gloves. He runs in and grabs them, but when he returns, she hasn't finished getting the horse ready. He takes her gloves and strikes her with them while scolding her for taking so long. She warns him that this is the first time he has stuck her and that he cannot do it two more times. Soon after, they arrive at the wedding. During the ceremony, she begins to sob loudly. Embarrassed, her husband angrily taps her arm. She tells him that the reason she is crying is because she can see how this marriage will end in heartbreak and ruin. She warns him this is the second time he has struck her and not to strike her a third time.

Now the shepherd loved the beautiful Lake Lady and took great care to not strike her again. Years passed and they had to attend a funeral. While the service was taking place she began to laugh joyfully and loudly. Startled and embarrassed the shepherd aggressively tapped her on her arm in an attempt to get her to stop. She looked at him with deep sadness in her eyes. She told him that she was laughing because she could see the spirit of the person who had just passed away. She could see how happy and free they were now. She immediately got up and went back to the lake. All the cows from her dowry and their offspring followed her to the lake and returned to their subaquatic realm. It was said that she would be seen again throughout the years. She would come to the surface of the water and teach her sons about the knowledge of herbs and healing remedies.

There are other stories about these Lake Ladies. Rather than in mythology, they are found in Welsh Folklore. These Lake Ladies are called the Gwragedd Annwn which translates to

English as "Wives of the Underworld" In these stories the Lake Ladies also have a connection to cows. One such story tells us of a Lake Lady who gifted a white cow to a farmer. This cow was special and brought much abundance to the land in the way of an ever-flowing supply of milk and abundant offspring. The farmer loved and took care of the cow for many years until one day he decided that it was old and should go to the butchers. The next day he took the cow to the butchers. When the butcher's axe came down on the head of the cow it did not die. Rather the axe was stuck in its head. It reared up and destroyed the butcher's shop.

Just then a loud scream could be heard from the cliff overlooking the lake where the lake lady lived. She began to scream with rage and call her sacred cow back home. The cow came running to the lake and went in. Like the story above, it was followed by its offspring and their offspring and so on. Until all the cows from that lineage had returned to the subaquatic realms of the Lake Lady. The village, now without any milk or cows, experienced a famine. The land grew barren and eventually, the village fell to ruin.

Another story of a Watery Maiden that has similar effects on the landscape is the story of the Well Maiden. Their story comes from a 13th-century poem called "The Elucidation". In this tale, we learn about the beautiful Well Maidens who were the voices of the wells. They lived in harmony with the land and were the voices of the well. This description may indicate they were oracles, are water spirits themselves, or both. The Well Maidens were beautiful, full of abundance, and were known to give food and water to anyone who passed by freely without exchange or payment. They did this until one day an evil king named King Amangon passed by. The King stopped and the Well Maiden gave freely of fresh spring water served in golden bowls and an abundance of food served on silver platters. The King and his men took the water and food from them. The King was evil, and he immediately lusted after the Well Maiden who was so generous. He gave in to his desire to have her. So, with force, he kidnaped the Well Maiden, stole her golden bowl, assaulted her, and forced her to serve only him. When his men saw this happen, they followed suit and kidnapped and assaulted the other Well Maidens. The remaining Well Maidens saw what had happened and retreated into the wells. The voices of the wells went silent, and the water ceased to flow. Because of this, the land fell into famine, it dried up, and everything shriveled and died. The land fell to ruin and became a barren wasteland.

Later in the poem, we learn that King Arthur's knights set off to find the Well Maidens in an effort to protect them and restore the wells. However, they don't find what they are looking for exactly. Rather they venture deep into the forest and find beautiful women who are protected by knights. These knights are fierce and fight off anyone who tries to approach the maiden. King Arthur's knights eventually capture one of these knights and take him back to court to surrender to King Arthur. When they do, the captured knight reveals the truth. The Well Maiden somehow escaped the clutches of the evil king and hid in the forest for years and years. They had children and raised them as knights to protect them. The Well Maidens learned how to heal themselves. They lived in a forest, a place that was abundant and they took the pain and trauma that they experienced and transformed it into something that would protect them. The land flourished, and the trees grew tall. They found abundance again in the realm of the forests and with their offspring who became their guardians.

The greed of men and their selfish desires for pleasure have always been costly for women in the human and subaquatic worlds. The desire of men seems to always come before the basic needs of women. From the beginning of time till the modern day, women have been harmed because men choose their pleasure over our well-being. They constantly risk our safety in pursuit of their selfish wants and desires. They often risk our safety or are the perpetrators of violence against our bodies and souls. They wish to possess us, control us, lock us up, and keep us hidden as if we are some object to be obtained. The result is the lack of fertility, abundance, sovereignty, and the creation of the barren wasteland. Rather than being in harmony with the landscape which is evident by the pollution and destruction of the land. It is our bodies that suffer. They are worked to depletion, betrayed, abused, harmed, and manipulated.

However, if we look at the stories of the Lake Lady and the Well Maiden, we see that they both had the courage to leave, to return to their subaquatic realms, and to restore balance within themselves. We also see in both stories these subaquatic magical maidens became mothers. They taught their sons the arts of healing. The Lake Ladies in the form of herbal remedies. The Well Maiden in the form of protection. Thus, ending the cycle of abuse that was perpetuated upon them. From a modern perspective, we can call upon the wisdom of these Watery Women to aid us in our own healing. I have experienced two different profound healing journeys with these subaquatic spirits that not only healed me but brought about massive change and transformation.

When I first began on a magical path I learned how to meditate. It wasn't long after that I decided to try to meditate in my bathtub. I soon found myself slipping into deep journeys and traversing the astral and subaquatic realms. Now whenever I am in a warm tub of water I can slip into an altered state and cross the hedge with ease. On one of these occasions, I had a healing experience with the Well Maiden I will never forget.

I was in the process of healing deep trauma. I had been reading and researching healing, I was practicing self-reiki every day. I was also doing rituals and spells for healing. It was during this time of active healing that this healing experience with the Well Maiden took place. One night I took a nice relaxing warm bath. It didn't take long for me to slip into the otherworld. I was a bit desperate back then. I wanted to heal but no matter what I did I couldn't quite clear the wounded energy from my body. I remember calling out in desperation. I screamed into the abyss and a group of beautiful watery women came to me. I think there were nine but to be honest I never counted them. I watched as they took my body and laid it down on a slab of stone. One of them shot light from her fingers and sliced me open from chest to pelvis in a straight line. I remember seeing them gather around, crack me in half, and open me up. They all began reaching inside of me. They were furiously working on me and moving things around inside of me. Then they began removing a thick, black, tar-like substance. It was sticky and there was so much of it. They used large arm movements as it was long and stretchy. Eventually, they gathered it all up and removed it. When it was all gone, they sealed me up without a scar and sat me up. They then told me I could call upon them for healing at any time.

A few years later I had another healing experience happened. This time it took place in an astral lake in the subaquatic realms. Again, I was in my bathtub. This time it was a ritual bath. I wasn't desperate for healing. I was in a great place in my life. I was grounded and I had regular meditation and ritual practice. I set up a beautiful bath with candles and herbs. I sunk in and began to journey. I journeyed to the edge of a cave and followed it down into the earth. When I came out to the other side, I found myself lakeside in the astral realm. I went into the water and was floating on my back. Then I felt several hands come up from the water below and wrap around my waist. I immediately felt myself being pulled down under the water. I didn't panic, there was a sense of calm and knowing and I surrendered to the downward flow. I was pulled down, deep into the water where the light was dim and hazy. This group of watery women suspended me in the water vertically. They began to work on my body as if I was a car and they were expert mechanics. They opened my head, cracked it open like they were rebuilding an engine, and placed a copper object into my head. It looked like a cross between a porthole window and a telescope. It was obvious to me that they had not only healed my body but enhanced my third eye in some way. It was such a profound experience that I will never forget it. From that moment forth I didn't need to journey to communicate with them. I have been in constant contact since. They have aided me in deep healing and continue to walk by my side as guides.

These intriguing watery women can help us to heal, learn balance, implement boundaries, and find sovereignty. There are many ways to work with them. One is through meditation and journey work others are through ritual and spell work. Working with these Watery Women can bring about transformation and profound healing. To do this you will want to begin by forming a relationship with them. One great way to do that is to dedicate time, energy, and space to them. A great way to do all three at once is by building an altar that you can dedicate to them. This becomes the perfect place to then spend time in ritual and meditation communing with them.

Creating an altar for the Lake Ladies or Well Maiden can be a beautiful way to get to know them better. It is also an act of devotion. It becomes an offering and can be a very rewarding process. Once you have selected your surface you will begin by anointing it with water. If you are dedicating it to the Lake Ladies use lake water. If it is to the Well Maiden use Spring water. If you have access to one of these bodies of water visit it and retrieve a small vial of water. Be sure that the water is safe to take and not contaminated. Bring this home and take a ritual vessel and place spring or tap water in it. Then take three drops of the lake or spring water you have collected and add it in. Hold your hands over the ritual vessel and visualize the Watery Women you wish to connect with. When you have the image clearly in your mind take a deep breath and blow your breath over the ritual vessel. As you do this, see the image in your mind become infused into the water with the power of your breath. If you do not have access to lake or fresh spring water, you can make a modification by infusing tap water with the image of a lake or spring. First place a clear glass bowl over an image of a lake or sacred spring. Then pour tap water into the bowl and then use the same visualization and breath process above. You can enhance this water by adding quarts or more folkloric elements like silver, hag stone, or ammonite. All three of which are used to create charmed healing waters.

Once you have prepared your water, wash the surface of the altar with this water. Take a white washcloth and dip it into the water. Then hold it over the surface of your altar space and squeeze it three times over the altar surface. In a sunwise manner start on the outer edge and in a large swirl pattern move the cloth inwards to the center. As you do visualize this becoming a beautiful space where you can connect with these Watery Women. Once this is done use a clean dry white towel to pat it gently dry.

Once this is done select an altar cloth if you wish to have one. I tend to choose blues and greens that look like water or that are similar colors to the bodies of water I work with. However, use what color you feel is best and what speaks to you. Once this is done you will want to find a sacred vessel. I recommend a bowl, but a chalice will also work. This will be the central part of your altar and will be a representation of a Lake or Sacred well. This is also a great place to scry and speak with the spirit of water. Place the vessel in the center front of your altar. If you are working with Lake Ladies, you may wish to add a mirror to the bottom of the bowl to capture its reflective nature. A simple way to do daily rituals is to pour water into the vessel in the mornings when you wake up. It keeps the life force alive, and the energy flowing. It can be a great and simple offering to these Watery Women. It is also a place where you can scry, pray, and commune with them to receive messages or their blessing. You may also wish to decorate your altar space with statues or figures of these Watery Women, candles, ammonites, plants from your local environment, and whatever you feel compelled to add.

A Sacred Bath to Heal with the Well Maiden or Lake Ladies

You will need...

White Rose Petals.
Lavender, Rosemary, Chamomile.
1 cup of Epsom Salts.
3 Quarts points.
Mortar and Pestle.
Gold Colored Bowl (or your chosen sacred vessel).
Offerings of fresh fruit and Springwater.
Candles to decorate your bathroom.
A few drops of Rosemary Essential Oil.

First, you will take your Lavender, Rosemary, and Chamomile and place them in a mortar and pestle. Grind them up using a circular sunwise motion. When this is done place the herbs into your golden bowl. Add your Epsom salt and stir the mixture together again using a sunwise direction. When this is done add a few drops of Rosemary Essential Oil and continue to stir. As you stir visualize yourself completely healed, balanced and sovereign. When it is mixed to your satisfaction flatten the salt and herb mixture and using your finger write the word "Healed" on top. Place the three quartz points into the salt to amplify the energy.

Next, go to your bathroom and begin filling your tub with water. As you do this light any candles you have and set the space to your liking. When the water is to the right temperature and depth take your salt and herb mixture and pour it into the bathtub in a sunwise direction. Using your hand stir the water, salt, and herbs one last time. As you do this visualize yourself balanced, healed, and sovereign one more time. Then take your white rose petals and sprinkle them into the bathtub. When you are ready get into your bath, relax, and allow yourself to slip into a meditative state. Visit the sub-aquatic or astral realms and commune with the Lake Ladies or Well Maiden and ask them for healing. Surrender to their magic and allow the healing waters and these subaquatic healers to do their work. When you are finished. Allow all the water to drain. Return the rose petals to the earth and place fresh fruit and spring or lake water on their altar as an offering and thanks for the work they have done.

Well Maiden Correspondences
Golden and silver platter
Golden Bowls
Bacon, Meat Pie, Bread
White towel
Food
Wells, Springs, and Founts
Forests
Knights

Lake Lady Correspondences
Lakes and Lake Water
Cows
Bread
Herbal Knowledge
Herbal Healing

Hera Under the Gaze of the God

Monica Gobbin

"…One day, Zeus, the King of the Gods, was walking around the beautiful region of Hesperides when he suddenly spotted Hera and fell head over heels in love with her.

To approach Hera, Zeus transformed himself into a cuckoo bird and placed himself outside her window, pretending to be frozen by the cold.

When Hera saw the little bird, she took pity on it. She nestled the little creature in her bosom to dry it, give it warmth, and take it inside her house.

At that moment, Zeus transformed back into his proper form, and Hera couldn't help it. She fell in love with him. When he asked her to be his wife this time, she obliged.

Then, he grabbed Hera and brought her to the mountain of Cithaeron to make her his legal wife so that she could cover her shame.

That marked the beginning of a vicious cycle of lust, infidelity, jealousy, and vengeance that would be the cornerstone of their relationship."

What does this story hide, a "love ruse" or a rape disguised with a poetic story?

The married life of Hera and Zeus is openly known for the extramarital adventures of the King of Olympus, for whom there were no limits to approaching any woman, mortal or immortal, even in the case of his divine wife. And this image of Hera does not represent the "good wife" of the ancient Greek world. Aristotle himself repeated the rules from *On a Good Wife* from Oikonomikos:

> "Not only taking care of the household economy, not allowing anyone in without her husband's knowledge, not getting into gossip or fights with other women, or listening to things that divert her from her main task: making her husband happy, pleasing him in all areas."

However, Hera did not comply with any of these rules....

And so, throughout their tumultuous married life, Hera's relationship with her children, stepchildren, and lovers of Zeus was the source of many myths. Her personality was taking violent and vengeful edges. Always faithful to her divine husband, she became the "caricature" of the deceived, embittered, and vindictive wife, who paradoxically cannot avoid the extramarital outrages of the god of law and order. The Queen of Olympus was unprotected from the actions of her husband. And her wounds are many and profound.

Since the publication of Dr. Shinoda Bolen's seminal book in the 90s, *Goddesses in Everywoman*, working with the archetypes of Greek goddesses has been widely disseminated in women's groups, within and outside of what is known as Feminine Spirituality.

How can we heal our wounds through these ancient myths that shaped our roles in our culture? The first step is to recognize ourselves in these old stories and release the emotions of anger, sadness, and helplessness embedded in our souls and psyches. For this, the best guide is the Goddess, who leads us to review our deep strata and recesses. The dark face of the Goddess looks deeply at us and, with her finger, points to the place where the wound is.

My job as a therapist is a significant area within my calling as a Priestess of the Goddess. The beginning of my work with

Goddess archetypes began with the Greek pantheon and Jean Shinoda Bolen. It was interesting to discover how most women identify with Pallas Athena, Aphrodite, or Artemis. Some felt like Hestia. But almost none of them thought of a preference for Hera, not even a minimum feeling of sympathy.

Hera is the ultimate spouse of the King of the Olympians. As such, she has sovereign power, but, on the other, She is also a troublesome deity who never ceases to question the decisions of her husband, who sets traps for him and hurls challenges at him. All this without adding the torments she inflicts on the other women who are the object of Zeus's desire and the children they bear him. Is she the antecedent of the evil stepmother of fairy tales?

Where did that antipathy come from? What would be the origin of that disgust towards that angry personality that most women did not fully understand then? Today, thirty years later, we can say that this feeling of rejection has two explanations. The first is that it manifests our shadow, which comprises feelings repressed in our unconscious. The second is cultural; this "jealous and angry wife" was the antithesis of the "good wife" that shapes patriarchal culture. It is interesting to highlight that Hera's rage does not point at her unfaithful husband; instead, She chased "the other woman" (who often had been seduced, raped, or deceived by Zeus) at children conceived by Zeus or innocent bystanders. (Shinoda Bolen, J. 2014)

In the portrait of Hera, which one finds in most mythological dictionaries, the anger, which is one of her characteristics, is usually attributed to the jealousy she feels for the extramarital relations of her spouse. From this point of view, the anger of Hera is the natural consequence of her married status and the prerogative of the legitimate spouse. The Goddess pointed always to act and primarily defend marriage as an institution. Which would be a fundamental and straightforward answer.

Hera was the heiress of an old Mediterranean Great Goddess who was always in the company of a subordinate consort. Zeus was the master of the new patriarchal order into which Goddess Hera could never comfortably integrate. In diachronic analyses, the jealousy and anger of Hera reveals that She was initially a formidable goddess in her own right who had difficulty fitting in with the Olympian pantheon.

As I expressed before, this interested me greatly. I tried to unravel the metamorphosis that the Goddess Hera suffered through the cultural transformation that resulted in establishing a patriarchal system in the culture. It was the way to free the Healing power that She possesses. On the Path to returning her greatness, She helps us heal from our shared wounds.

Let's go step by step.

Hera: Her Origins in Archaic Greece

History tells us that every time myths explain a war between the pantheons of gods, there has been a conquest where the gods of the victors defeat the gods of the dominated. Sometimes, certain cults are so deeply rooted in the towns that, over time, relationships grow between them. Classical Greece is a good example, where the primal Goddesses became into the roles of Wife, Daughter, and Sister of one male God, and often Her attributions transferred to the male deity. Religion is a significant factor in determining and sustaining the behaviors of society. From an anthropological point of view, myths have a "pedagogical" function: to shape expected behaviors.

The dominant presence of a Goddess in the pantheons of Mesopotamia, Anatolia, and the Eastern Mediterranean began to dilute and have changed at some point. The figure of the Mother Goddess metamorphosed under the hegemony of Zeus and the inhabitants of Olympus, the third-generation gods. The attributes of the Great Goddess became the different qualities of the Greek goddesses. Those Goddesses are Gaia, Rhea, Hekate, Hera, Hestia, Demeter and Persephone, Athena, Artemis, and Aphrodite). However, all those figures, features, and characters are the derivatives of the same archetype. (Kortanoğlu, E., 2020) With Hera, however, this power comes to an end.

The metaphor of an Olympian family of gods presumably entered Greek consciousness in the misty Dark Ages that separated the Bronze and Archaic periods. It crystallized, however, as the way Greeks pictured their gods in the late eighth century when *The Iliad* was finally reaching its final shape. By this early Archaic period, Zeus' power in the mythical realm was secure, and threats of rebellion by Hera and other deities belonged to a remote past. We are talking about the period of Panhellenism when local and regional myths and rites began to take on a patriarchal color by the "Panhellenic Homer," who adapted the local ritual for the Panhellenic epic.

In many ways, Hera's role in Greek mythology is ironic. However, the Goddess of women could not prevent them from sleeping with her husband, her husband, who was constantly committing adultery despite Hera's being the Goddess of marriage. Despite his infidelities, she stood by him, though at times, his actions wound her and consumed her with anger and rage. Hera became increasingly erratic and unpredictable, unleashing all manner of punishments on his lovers and their offspring.

During an early stage of the cult, primarily before 600 B.C.E., Hera was viewed as a goddess of general fertility. She was a goddess linked to the earth, Nature, and renewal processes. During a later stage, primarily after 600 B.C.E., she was viewed as the sister-wife of Zeus. The Goddess with sovereignty over all life came to be understood mainly as a goddess of familial domestication. (O'Brien, J., 1993)

In Hesiod's *Theogony*, we're told that Hera was the youngest daughter of Kronos and Rhea, king and queen of the Titans.

The Titans themselves were offspring of the primal gods Gaia (Earth) and Ouranos (Sky), so Hera was in the third generation of the gods, known as the Olympians. She was the wife and sister of Zeus, the king of the gods, and the mother of several major deities, including Ares, Hephaestus, and Eileithyia. Hera was associated with marriage, fertility, childbirth, and women's roles in general and was also considered a protectress of cities and states. She served as queen of the gods and the Goddess of childbirth and marriage. Hera was the sister of Zeus, as well as his wife. As did most Greek gods, she lived on Mount Olympus.

Hera/Juno was the Goddess of marriage and children's birth, so she was honored to the utmost importance. It protected women from birth to death. She was sometimes called "the Lady." She appears in the company of a peacock and carries a grenade in her left hand and a scepter in the right, which relates Her to an older Goddess of the Dead. Hera/Juno ruled all rites and preparations for marriage. The calendar was also governed and used the menstrual cycle to symbolize the passage of time. She leads the "Calends," the first day of the lunar month. She was the Goddess of the Holy Union.

Hera had several sacred animals: peacock, cuckoo, and cow. Sometimes, Hera holds a rod topped by a pomegranate – a symbol of fertility – along with a cuckoo. Other times, She rides a chariot driven by peacocks. The Greeks believed the peacock's feathers symbolized her watchfulness and all-seeing Nature. Also, one of Hera's symbols was the cow, sometimes depicted with cow horns or a cow by her side. In some versions of the myth, Hera took on the form of a cow to hide from Zeus. In some myths, Hera has the power to control the weather, including causing thunderstorms and hailstorms.

Despite her importance in Greek religion, Hera was also known for her turbulent relationship with Zeus, her husband and brother. Hera's marriage to Zeus was far from a happy one. She was often jealous of Zeus's infidelities and his children with other women and was known for her vengeful nature. She was also a key player in many myths and legends, including the Trojan War, where she supported the Greeks against the Trojans.

What would be the actual cause of the turbulent relationship with Zeus? We could express two reasons for different levels here. First, Hera was a local deity of great power, the Goddess of the Sky, the Earth, beasts, and fertility in women and livestock. After the Indo-European invasions, a new pantheon was structured with a god as father and king. And the Goddess is forced to be his wife, ashamed of how he has taken her. Zeus raped Her. This anger accompanying the loss of sovereignty and physical and emotional abuse does not dilute; it accompanies her for the rest of her existence. This situation would represent what many women from native families had to go through before the conquerors. How Hera treats the children of Zeus also implies the fight to eliminate heirs of the new order. However, this "war" between them does not prevent them from recognizing the images of the Sacred Matrimony, re-enacting the old ritual marriage of Heaven and Earth, which blessed and regenerated Life.

But shouldn't we limit Hera to her status as an "angry and jealous wife"? We should understand that even though the concept of a couple or marriage has evolved, we still have reasons to continue feeling anger because physical, mental, and emotional abuse by people around us, not just our boyfriends or husbands, is still a sad reality. "The unseemly squabbling between Zeus and Hera is the outcome, not of conjugal jealousy, but of racial rivalry. Hera remains always the turbulent native princess, coerced but never really subdued by the alien conqueror." (Harrison, J. 1928)

From this perspective, we can see the theme of rage more broadly than the condition of "Zeus's jealous wife." Goddess Hera's anger is a reaction to the attack on her position and body. A response to the "theft" of her attributes and power. To the insult and deterioration of her sovereignty. In the 21st century, the social need to marry and have children is no longer a priority for many women. So is the fact of remarriage with "exes" and stepchildren. However, we tend to be highly vulnerable to abuse in many environments.

What Do the Stories of the Wounded Goddesses Give Us?

Archetypes are guiding principles in the hidden part of the human psyche; They are fields and centers of force that serve to order any element that sinks into the unconscious. According to Jolande Jacobi (1971):

> "...all expressions of life, to the extent that they are of a general and typical human type, rest on an archetypal foundation, regardless of whether they manifest themselves in the biological, the psychobiological or the mental."

But a clear distinction must be made between archetype in the sense of the potentiality to take shape and archetype in understanding a possibility that had already taken form: the archetypal image. Literature often emphasizes the latter. This issue has been one of the many sources of confusion in the information circulating.

The Origin of Hera's Anger: Abuse or Infidelity?

Throughout history, the literature about Zeus has always praised him without a hint of criticism about his predatory behavior towards goddesses and humans. As father and king of the gods, his power was absolute. A divine family organization endorsed the patriarchal social system materialized in the Olympic family. What's more, in many books where the myth with which this essay begins is detailed, rape is poetically covered up under a kind of passionate impulse.

We can see through other myths that the rivalry between Hera and Zeus was not limited to their reactions to his infidelities. In *The Iliad*, we can point out three moments in which Zeus threatens physical punishment of Hera:

- When Hera inquiries about what happens between Zeus and Thetis, concerning Achilles (remember that Thetis was Zeus's partner). When at Hera's instigation, she and Pallas Athena intervene in a battle on behalf of the Achaeans. After Zeus's deception by Hera.

It's hard to expect any other kind of reaction from Hera. We must understand this from the perspective of someone who has suffered abuse and abuse for a lifetime.

To overthrow Zeus, Hera decided to drug Zeus and make him fall asleep. Once asleep, the gods tied Zeus to his throne. As Zeus awoke, he was furious and began arguing with the gods who bound him to the throne. Briareus, also known as Aegaeon, was a giant with 100 arms and 50 heads.

He overheard the arguments and came to help Zeus. He could untie the knots that the gods had tied when binding Zeus to the throne. Once Zeus was free, he grabbed his iconic thunderbolt and threatened to strike down the gods who had bound him. The gods begged for their lives, and Zeus showed mercy on them, but he did not forgive his wife.

As punishment for her attempt to overthrow him, Zeus seized Hera and hung her in the sky by golden chains. Hera wailed in pain all night, but no one would help her out of fear of Zeus.

After getting no sleep that night, Zeus approached Hera the following day and agreed to take her off the chains if she promised she would never go against him. Hera reluctantly had to agree to be released from the chains, but she continued to use her cleverness against Zeus any chance she got.

We can see here the subsequent subjugation of Hera before the absolute power of her husband. She has her ambitions and plans and is not simply the "obedient wife" you might expect. I imagine Hera's feelings and subsequent resentment. The poets caricatured the image of the Great Goddess Hera so that people would forget the power that She had in the past. In almost the same way that Western culture has caricatured feminism.

Rape, Abuse, and Loss of Self-Esteem and Personal Power

Rape has always been a part of human culture. The myths of antiquity included accounts of rape; ancient societies counted rape among the crimes listed in their law codes, and even the Bible contains stories of rape. Throughout the centuries, rape has impacted individual women (as well as men and children of both sexes). Still, it has also affected the evolution and development of cultures worldwide, as women have been abducted as brides, claimed as prizes of war, and enslaved. Unfortunately, rape remains a concern of modern life. (Smith, D. 2004, p 6).

Over time, the denigration of the Great Primal Goddess was reflected in a series of myths in many cultures, where the Goddess is attacked, injured, or dismembered. The theme of rape in the Greek pantheon reflects a cruel reality that women suffer.

Rape culture forces women to seek safe environments, which leads them to sacrifice improvements in work or professional terms. It is often not only the physical threat but also the emotional and intellectual threats. All of this is at the root of feminine anger, of which Hera is a symbol if we open our eyes.

The issue of guilt, devaluation, and the reaction of non-victim third parties joined the physical and emotional trauma of rape. From culture, there are "myths" that also provide a negative charge. For example: "Women tend to exaggerate how it affects them…", "She probably provoked him…", "She drinks alcohol and wears tight clothes…" etc. All these beliefs tend to punish the victim.

We have reached a time when it is necessary to recognize women's anger and overcome fears of expressing their reasons. The first step to healing We carry within us the wrath of the Goddess Hera. But this anger should not lead us down a destructive path; it should be the sign that there is a Divine Wound within us, and only through healing them can we achieve the healing of the feminine collective. And this process must be understood from another definition of power, community, and person. Meaning of power from the religion of the Goddess, where each person is free to choose the Path

Healing the Anger with Hera

Although today we can find various materials that present ways of working with Hera by accessing the sources of multiple authors who work with Goddess archetypes, I wish to contribute some ideas for Goddess Healing, emphasizing the theme of "anger" and abuse – the impact of Zeus's abuse of Her and the continued erosion of Her Sovereignty.

Connecting with Hera

One of the ways that can help us connect with Hera is to get closer to her myths and images and give her a space in our lives. An altar is a sacred space between the Goddess and us. Knowing her Symbols will bring us closer to Her.

Ideas for setting up an altar

- Colors: Greenish blue- Pink- White/royal blue/purple items (cloth, candles)

- Gems: Rose Quartz – Chrysoprase – Emerald – Jade – Kunzite – Pink Opal – Rhodochrosite – Pink Tourmaline – Citrine – Garnet – Diamonds – pearls and amber (even if they are not minerals).Incenses: Bergamot-Jasmine – Lavender – Nardo – Rose – Ylang-ylang – Jasmine – Iris – Myrrh, civet
- Herbs-Woods: Angelica – Juniper – Mint – Yarrow – Elderberry – Uva ursi – Verbena
- Flowers: Copa de Rey – Gardenia – Gladiolus – Hydrangea – Primroses – Pink – Tulip
- White flowers: Lilies – Irises – Lotus – Waterlilies.
- Objects: Diadem – Something representing the seasons of the year – shed peacock feathers- Depictions/photos/art of cows, cuckoo, eagles, peacocks, lions, crabs, snails – Statues of Her – Leaves or bark from cypresses or maple trees – Cuckoo clocks – Depictions/imagery of thrones
- Metals: Silver – Platinum – Gold
- Offering: Milk – Pomegranates – Honey

You can follow a tradition to assemble the Altar and arrange the objects. You can track your intuition if you do not belong to any.

Hera and Our Inner Anger

For a long time, our culture has instilled in us that feeling anger and rage is not typical of women. This belief has led countless of them to suppress it instead of looking for healthy ways to free themselves from toxic emotions. In this way, in many of us, these emotions are deposited in an underground layer, distorting our being over the years.

The environment tells us to forget and move on even when this emotion is justified. But can we continue with that burden? Isn't it dragging a weight that prevents us from moving forward? I see it as a thorn in the nail that, as time goes by, takes the shape of a boil. However, feeling anger can be the indicator, the symptom that we must heal something profound. Anger shows us exactly where we are hurt so that we can prioritize working on that part of our lives. The dissolution of anger can begin with us from the self-empathy we can offer ourselves. Connecting with the emotions in the body and our sensations is vital.

Of course, we are never letting this anger control us. Anger can become the guide to empowerment thanks to Hera's guidance. If you can find the courage to slow down and look at what is underneath your anger, you may find yourself quickly in touch with the most hurting, wounded, and vulnerable parts of yourself. Maybe we will find our previous girl there, full of fury and pain for the injustices suffered, the abuse, and not being cared for and protected.

Perhaps this anger is focused on one person we blame for all of this. We may have been in a relationship with a narcissistic or psychopathic person. But staying there won't help us. Nor should we remain in the feeling of guilt. Moving from that place involves conscious and sustained work.

When a person experiences trauma, their identity goes through a process of fragmentation where painful feelings are kept hidden until a safe space for expression is provided.

That is why we will stop ignoring it or resorting to pills (literal or metaphorical) to avoid pain. It is also possible that the feeling is confusing, and we do not know exactly where it comes from. Damage from the past can remain in those underground layers, sending symptoms that we do not know how to decipher. Or literally, make our bodies sick.

That's because the struggle against difficult emotions is a war against us.

How should we proceed?

Get into a position where you don't feel discomfort but aren't completely relaxed. Close your eyes and monitor your breathing. Once you've sufficiently slowed your breathing, start to remember your last episode of anger.

The first step is to recognize that feeling of anger, its origin, and how we handle it. Pay close attention to what the anger you hold is telling you. As you pay attention to your anger, ask yourself these questions:

Very briefly describe the situation.

What makes you angry (Is it an abusive relationship? something painful that happened in the past? etc.) Am I angry at myself or someone else (or both)?

What emotions connect to that anger (hurt, disappointment, fear, etc.)? Has the anger turned into something else (like rage or bitterness)?

After attempting to address it, based on your anger, is it getting worse or better?

Identifying the source of the anger:

Is there an area where I don't feel safe or free to be ultimately me?

Are there needs not being met (emotionally, physically, spiritually, financially, etc.)?

Am I making the situation worse for myself in some way?

Addressing the situation causing the anger:

What one step can I take to address the problem causing my rage?

If I've tried to address the situation already, is there a different way to handle it that might help?

Do I need someone else's perspective or help to address the situation or anger (therapist, friend, etc.).

Write your thoughts in your journal. After that, you can write a letter to Hera or a prayer to ask her for help and guidance messages. Then, put the paper on the Altar at the feet of her image.

Raise a card from our Tarot or Oracle.

Close the ritual.

You can do the ritual whenever you want. But the best time is the night before the New Moon, when the old cycle will end, and the energy is cleansing and closure.

Hera and Our Sacred Renewal:

Cleansing Ritual Baths are magnificent spiritual tools. In this case, it is a very ancient ritual linked to Hera. It can help us heal from abuse. It is essential to set a purpose, as in any practice, whether to cleanse myself of toxic emotions or to renew my energy. Water is cleansing, healing, restoring, and refreshing. Or you can also incorporate it into your birthday celebrations.

Although it can be done at any time, aligning it with the corresponding phase of the Moon gives it a potent force. You can do it every New Moon if you want to renew yourself. If you need to "purge," do it on Full or Waning Moons.

Following the purpose of the Ritual Bath, we will add certain flowers, oils, or gems to the bath water, always considering the side effects they may have. We must use essential oils suitable for placing on the skin. And remember that not all flowers or gems can be inert. Many can provoke reactions in us. Chamomile and Lavender are safe, as well as quartz. You can put the flowers and the herbs in a bag of muslin or tulle. You can also prepare an infusion and pour it into the water.

The remains must be buried in the garden or a pot after the ritual.

You can begin with the ritual steps using the bathing area. Always prepare an altar and incense. Your bath area symbolises the crossing of two streams of water where Hera performed her ritual bath. Visualise this place where she and you meet.

One way to do it is to enter the bathtub or shower with an image of Hera. Or, if you prefer, begin the ritual with ablutions to her statuette while saying a prayer related to the purpose of the Ritual Bath. The best invocations are the ones we create from the heart. Then you can place it where you can see it when you enter the bath water.

In the water, visualise how the Goddess helps you cleanse or renew yourself. Feel how she connects to you and guides you. Take it if you ever can do it in a river or the ocean.

Although each person has their bathing habits, as well as the way to dry themselves in a ritual bath, there are some excellent tips:

- To attract something into your Life? Wash and dry yourself from foot to head (upwards) to draw things to you.
- To rid yourself of something? Wash and dry from head to foot (downwards).
- To do a cleansing or uncrossing ritual bath, dry yourself from head to foot and fully clean the bathtub.
- To perform money or love drawing a bath or attracting something to you? Let yourself drip-dry instead of towel-drying off.

Hera and Our Relationships

She is a Goddess of the relationships where there is a commitment. She teaches us to open ourselves to ways of living as a couple without falling into co-dependency.

This guided visualization can be exceptional for New Moons in Libra or when the Moon is in that sign. It can be recorded and edited with music beforehand. The questions can help to elaborate on the "seeds" intentions for new moons in Libra.

Find a comfortable position. With one hand on the chest and another on the abdomen, inhale deeply through the nose, ensuring that the diaphragm (not the chest) inflates with enough air to widen the lungs. Do it slowly. Take ten slow breaths.

Allow your arms and legs to relax. Wrap yourself in a bubble of white light to feel in a protected and safe space to embark on our journey.

If something breaks into your mind, eliminate it with your breath. Pay attention to any physical sensation that appears during this visualization.

Slowly breathe while you feel that your body becomes lighter and lighter. It is so weightless that it starts to float, and you can go out the window towards the beautiful night sky, full of stars. It's the New Moon and the time of Hera-Juno.

You keep floating until you reach the Milky Way. Your body is so light that you can glide, saluting the millions of stars that make up the galaxy.

You turn around and see the imposing time on his throne of Heaven. There she is, waiting for you. Hundreds of Lapis Lazuli fragments form her dress and mantle. With its Animals of Power, the Sacred Cow, whose milk gives rise to the stars, and the peacock, whose "eyes" look at Eternity.

You approach gently, and She extends Her hand to reach you and let you sit before the throne.

The Great Lady looks at you with sweetness, with Her Eyes so beautiful, and asks you what you need. It is as if She were there for you. She knows that in us, there is as much Light as Shadow and helps us to be able to open ourselves to love and commitment with a partner.

She says: Come and tell me …

Do you feel that your relationship with yourself is broken in your heart? Do you think that you are not "whole"? What's missing in your Life??

Have you found respect and commitment? The internal balance …?

Have you felt the anguish and pain in the face of infidelity?

Do you constantly compare yourself with other women? Do you distrust them constantly?

Do you feel that your jealousy is the symptom of an unmet need?

Do you feel that "others" are responsible for your unhappiness? Do you need the approval of others, even at the cost of your convictions? Do you forgive everything in order not to be left alone?

Are you looking for love?? What does love mean to you? Do you love yourself as you expect others to love you??

Review each of Goddess Hera's questions. Check what truths hide your heart. Ask the Goddess you need to bring happiness to this area of your Life.

Ask her what you need to keep your balance, the inner sacred marriage, to open yourself to a relationship that gives you the love you deserve.

Take your gift, a peacock feather that will allow you to move the things you need and balance the balance between you and your meaningful bond.

Take a deep breath and slowly make your way back.

Asking the Soul

- What do I need in the couple or the marriage? What do I need to strengthen through the relationship? What shortcomings do I seek to compensate for?
- What qualities define my inner partner? What aspects complement me?
- What are my values about the couple?

- What do I value in my current relationship?
- From Astrology, what can the Asteroid Juno offer us?

Karl Ludwig Harding discovered the asteroid Juno on 1 September 1804. It was the third asteroid found but was initially considered a planet; it was reclassified as an asteroid and minor planet during the 1850s.

The Roman Goddess, Juno, was the protector and counselor of the state who held watch over women. The Greek goddess counterpart was Hera, although Juno and Hera didn't have equivalent roles.

Considering Juno's impact on our chart, we can become more aware of our wounds around partnership and the more significant lessons surrounding relationship dynamics.

The asteroid placement in our natal astrology chart reveals our critical motivators for being in a relationship and our core attachment wounds.

Her importance was tied to her husband, Jupiter, the king of gods, and embodied traditional ideas of monogamy and marriage. But let us remember that the definitions of planetary factors reflect the concepts of Hellenistic Astrology, where the figure of Zeus-Jupiter is exalted and highlighted. Juno is the "jealous and angry wife" without cause or explanation. The primary idea of Wound, which is rape by her partner, is not considered.

It is interesting to note that I have found in birth charts of women raped by their partner a connection between the asteroid Juno and the asteroid of the "Victim," Dejanira, who was the wife of Heracles, raped by the centaur Nessus.

A look at feminine spirituality on the asteroid Juno should include a reflection on the wounds of the Goddess and not only analyze their manifestations, whether through anger, depression, jealousy, etc. Also, She teaches us how to heal our Wounds.

Blodeuwedd – Goddess of the Beautiful Wild

Halo Quin

Introduction – The Dance with the Wild Within

Created from the wild, returned to the wild, scorned for what she was not, Blodeuwedd (pronounced "blod-EYE-weth") is a mercurial figure arising from the green land of Wales, soaked in magic and often misunderstood.

Here I want to share with you some of my personal journey with this goddess. At least, she is a goddess to me. This is just one story of one person's relationship with her, and not to be taken as gospel, but I hope that in my dance with this beloved being you find keys to your own healing and understanding.

Blodeuwedd has guided me in healing and integration, and helped me to find perseverance to survive the pressures of life. You can read her story in *Y Mabinogi*, and a short version in my book, *Gods and Goddesses of Wales*. If you want to get to know any deity, I always recommend exploring their stories and lore, but throughout my account here I've offered up exercises to help you tune into her energy as I know her.

Sweet and wild in equal measure, to me she is the untamed truth and beauty of life.

Who Is Blodeuwedd?

Blodeuwedd is a figure from Welsh myth, specifically found in the fourth branch of *Y Mabinogi*. She has become a modern goddess for many pagans, though sometimes she's seen as a spirit, a fairy queen, or a wicked woman.

The story tells us that the Lleu Llaw Gyffes was born under difficult circumstances, leading to his mother, Arianrhod, to place him under a tynged (often described as a curse but it's more of a "fate") that he will only get a name if she names him. His uncle, the enchanter and trickster Gwydion, tricks her into naming the boy. Next a tynged that he'll only get weapons from her hand – and thus can only become a man in the eyes of society if she arms him. Again, Gwydion tricks her into giving the boy weapons. Finally, Arianrhod places him under a tynged that he will never marry a woman of human born. No easy trickery to solve this fate, Gwydion asks his uncle, the great magician Math, to help him create a woman for Lleu, and they conjure him a wife from the flowers of oak, broom, and meadowsweet. They name her "Blodeuedd" ("blod-EYE-eth") which simply meant "flowers".

Blodeuedd was a dutiful wife, but was never given a choice of who she would love. It was not uncommon for women to find themselves in a political or practical marriage rather than one where they chose their husband for love, but she was not a human, not truly, and so when she meets a man who treats her as an equal with agency, Gronw, she is not bound by the social norms in the way one might expect. Blodeuedd and Gronw plot to kill Lleu, and almost succeed, leading to Gronw's death at the hand of Lleu in retaliation, and Gwydion turning Blodeuedd into an owl as punishment, to be shunned by the other birds and to never again see the light of day. Her name becomes Blodeuwedd, "Flower-face", and is an old name for owls in Wales.

A Prayer Offered Freely
Blodeuwedd,
Flower-faced lady of the skies.
You who move between the worlds,
beyond limitations,
beyond expectations.

You who know the ways of roots and petals,
of feathers and talons,
the nature of Nature in light and dark.
We ask you to teach us to shift our shapes into who we
    are,
to know and follow our true loves,
and to embrace all possibilities that we may choose our
    freedom with joy.
Guide us to stay true to ourselves in all moments,
and show us the magic of life that weaves through all
    beings.
May we know our challenges in your story,
and see clearly the path through heartache to truth.
Blodeuwedd,
may your name and story be a blessing to all,
and may you know that you are loved.

Blodeuwedd's Story (a Retelling)

This is the story you won't find in the old manuscripts, seen through my eyes, the eyes of the wild blinking in the evening light.

It began with wanting, not ours, his. We did not want, we were.

Our leaves soaking up the warm light, roots bathed in soft soil, drinking in the rain, turning towards the sun. Part of that wide web of mycelium whispers singing through the land. Growing to the sun and dying to become the soil that nourishes in turn.

Then the magicians came and pulled us from our home, weaving their enchantments, shaping the world to their will. Shaping us into one.

They took flowers and made woman.

And we became me. Blodeuedd, Blossoms.

I was told I was beautiful, that I belonged to the little prince, the golden-haired man born of magic and bound by his mother's fate-weaving. I was given over to this strange world, strange place, no longer rooted but free to explore, dance, see in new ways. In his arms I felt things I'd never felt before, even while the voice of the land was muted.

I turned towards his light, until, one day, he left for a time.

And another came. Hair dark as a shadow at midnight, hunting with his folk and in need of shelter for the night.

This one didn't assume I was his, I welcomed him into my home and we met as equals.

It was then that I learned I was free to choose.

Society disagreed.

We plotted my escape from my husband – till death do us part. What is death to a flower? Simply a time to become soil, a time of change. What is death to a prince? Well, he became an eagle and flew away.

And yet, when the Magician discovered what we had done to his nephew he chased me and my women into the mountains, drowned them in a lake, and sought to punish me by turning me into an owl.

But perhaps he just set me free.

To choose, to love, to be wild... and owned only by me.

Exercise – Listening to the Flowers

(With thanks to Cristina Pandolfo, from whom I learned the formalised heart-communication method which I have adapted here.)

Blodeuwedd began her existence as flowers, as part of the green growing land of Wales, rich and damp and fertile with life. Nowadays we usually judge the morality of deities by human standards, but the story of Blodeuwedd offers us the opportunity to shift our perspective on life.

If you can, find a plant to sit with. A flowering plant is ideal. If you can't access one physically then set aside time where you'll be undisturbed and bring one to mind.

Approach with an open attitude, and the question of whether they're happy for you to sit with them for a time. Notice how you feel in response, and listen to that feeling. Discomfort is an indication that they don't want to be disturbed, a sense of welcome or lightness suggests that the answer is yes. For a living plant an offering of water or juice might be suitable, as a way of sharing with them. For an energetic-imaginary plant, then sending gratitude as a feeling is good.

Explore, in person or in your mind, the shape, colour, texture, scent of the plant.

Begin to notice the environment it is within. What is the soil like? Is there a lot of sunlight or a lot of shade? Is it by water or in a dry place?

Breathe into your heart and allow yourself to relax, to tune into that space of relating.

The heart is said to be a space where magnetic fields meet, and where information can be exchanged. Through the heart we can listen to the energy of the plants.

Imagine the energy centre of your heart expanding, softening, opening.

Where it meets the energy of the plant, allow the experience of the plant to be shared with you and notice what it feels like.

In this space of connection, you might ask the question, "what is life?"

Listen to how the plant responds.

Explore other questions if you choose, such as "what is love?" "what does it mean to die?" "What is freedom?" or others of your own devising. Allow plenty of time for responses, which may come into your understanding as words, feelings, images, scents, sounds, or other beings in the environment. The information and energy will be translated by your body-mind into something that you can receive, so notice and be open.

When you feel like it is time to stop, thank the plant and breathe into your heart, allowing that energy to settle back into yourself, and back into a size that is normal for you.

Take a moment to let the experience settle for you, and make any notes that you need to.

This is where Blodeuedd came from, how she began.

What does this experience tell you about the Goddess made of flowers?

Wild or Wicked?

Blodeuwedd is often presented as a wicked woman who betrayed her husband, who went against the role that she was supposed to play, and who was punished for it. *Y Mabinogi* is a collection from medieval manuscripts and so the beings described within are often magical, but are not labeled as deities. Rather they are described in terms of human behaviour, and judged as such.

I see Blodeuwedd in a different light. When she appears in circle, or I encounter her in the world, she is an untamed energy, a wild being, sovereign of herself. She is unapologetically what she is, and that is not simply human.

My first encounter with her was at a Reclaiming Witchcamp (a magical intensive retreat) where we were working with her story and there, we explored the idea that she was, throughout it all, the spirit of the wild embodied in different forms. Why would the consciousness that arises from flowers behave as a human would? Why would a flower worry about following social norms?

In the work of Kristoffer Hughes I learned of the nuance in the Welsh language which illuminates Gwydion as an illusionist, and when I looked deeper at the stories, this is true. Gwydion changes the appearance of things. Math can change the nature of things, and that is why Gwydion needs his help to make Blodeuedd, but when he turns her into an owl in the end, he is not changing her nature but revealing it: she is still a spirit of the wild.

The spirit of flowers is shaped into a human, and has human experiences. And then, she is transformed back into a creature, flying free.

Blodeuwedd, then, has magically lived in the plant, human, and bird realms. She knows the day, the night, and the in-between.

And she learned how to recognise a situation which she was trapped in, and how to do whatever was necessary to escape it.

Exercise – Welcoming the Goddess with an Altar

One wonderful way of getting to know a deity is to create an altar to invite them into your home. I like to think of the shrines on my altar as guest bedrooms for my gods and spirits, and creating a pleasing display with objects and symbols which resonate with the Goddess in question is a lovely way to make Her welcome. Start by reading her stories and thinking about what she might enjoy, and which aspect of her you want to connect with. You might focus on her as the spirit of the Flowers, connected to the land. Or perhaps you resonate with Blodeuedd, the Woman exploring human life, love, and pleasure, as well as discovering who she chooses to be and what lengths she'll go to be free to love. Or perhaps you feel the call to work with Blodeuwedd in her owl form, after she has learned who she is and integrated the human into the wild.

Flowers are ideal for an altar to this goddess. But rather than blossoms torn from the earth you could include potted flowers that you can tend, so that when you water or prune them (as best suits the flower you choose) you do so as an act of devotion to the nature spirit. Giving to our green friends rather than taking is a beautiful way of honouring this aspect of this Goddess. You might also choose to gather meadowsweet, broom, and oak, which are traditionally the flowers she was made of, or to use pictures of flowers.

What colours speak to you of the wild? I like a deep green for her, in all her faces, for the green world that she came from and returned to. I sometimes imagine her first steps with human toes into the rich green grass, discovering new sensations and possibilities.

Owls are her most obvious symbol. With their large watchful eyes taking in all of life, and their untamed hearts. You might choose an image of a tawny owl, native to her homeland of Wales, you might find an abstract owl statue, or one that is native in your landscape, bringing you closer to the wild spirit of the land you live on.

You might choose a scent which reminds you of freedom, or choice, of shapeshifting, or of the plant kingdom to drop onto a cloth on your altar, or to hang feathers in front of a picture that you can stroke as you go by. Remember to engage as many of your senses as you can, so that you're really bringing in her energy in as many ways as move you.

Flowers, owls, and the colours and scents of the natural world are great places to begin, and then see what items appear for you.

My altar to her is simple and includes a small brass owl, a Celtic knotwork picture painted in her honour with a tawny owl feather in the frame, and an owl candle holder. It is somewhere I can see it often, and so I'm often reminded of Blodeuwedd, her strength, and the challenges she kept me company through.

Choice, Escape, Being True to Oneself.

We can find ourselves trapped in situations in many ways, often by our own choices (but not always). Blodeuwedd is a goddess who, newly born as human, found herself in a marriage she had no choice in.

In my case, it was my own choices that led me there.

Once upon a time, I married a man who, while not cruel, was not right for me, who did not know how to be a partner. We were together for twelve years. Each year I asked myself "how long do I stay? How long do I wait for things to get better?"

It was never quite bad enough to leave, but something was wrong.

I sacrificed pieces of myself for the relationship. Putting my dreams on hold so he could pursue his. Believing his excuses for withholding love, affection, support. Working harder and carrying more of the relationship until my back spasmed and my body ached. One day, finally, I broke.

I had been working with Blodeuwedd for years, by then, flying with the owl to feel free of something I couldn't quite place my finger on. Rooting with the flowers and feeling the sunlight to remind me of the infinite love and power that flows through the earth. She kept showing up in my life and I wasn't sure why, but her presence helped me keep the thread of my own dreams and the deep knowing that there was more possible. Where you end up isn't where you have to stay, she told me.

She spoke to me of shapeshifting, of finding the truth of yourself no matter how you had to behave in the world. When we flew in visions I felt, under silent wings, the expanse of possibility beyond the daily grind. When I brewed tea from her flowers she whispered to me of the wisdom of the plant world.

Then, one evening, a truth was spoken and it hit me. He could not be a partner to me because, at its simplest, he did not see me as a partner, but as a means to an end. I made life easy for him, we weren't equals in the dance of life. As Lleu was in need of a wife to be seen as a man in the world, as he needed to marry the land to gain his sovereignty, so too had my husband married me because I was useful to him.

I want to be clear that it wasn't malicious on his part, just selfish. And I chose to stay, building that dynamic because it made me feel useful, needed, and whatever else I got out of self-sacrifice. But the outcome was still devastating.

When we sleepwalk into a relationship and stay out of co-dependence, when we are not partners, not equal, then we lose ourselves. I slowly lost myself.

Blodeuwedd whispered to me – fly away, fly away, remember who you are, who you can be, wild and free...

Eventually I listened.

Time has passed since then and this story has a happy ending. We're both doing much better in our lives and our selves. I, like Blodeuwedd, chose a new life for myself and found freedom and love elsewhere, with someone who knows me as an equal and treats me like a partner. But she also taught me that I am whole in myself, capable of flying free regardless of relationships, and worthy of freedom as well as support.

With the flowers I root and bask in the sun. With the owl I fly, my power to hunt my dreams my own or with those I choose.

Exercise – Lessons from the Owls

Depending on where you live it might be easy for you to wait quietly outside at night and listen to the owls, or it might be a huge challenge. If you can, listening to the owls call in the night is a powerful experience. The owls I've lived near here in Wales are tawny and barn owls, so let me share a little of them with you.

Tawny owls make the "Twuit-twhoo" call that I learned as a child, and this is actually two owls calling and answering each other. One calls "Twuit" and the other replies "twhoo". When you hear this, you know the owls are speaking softly to each other – "are you there?" "I'm here." "You are not alone." For me it is a sound of relating and connecting. Even in the night, even far from the sun, there is warmth.

Barn owls have sharp voices, their cries cutting through the night, just like their white feathers slice through the dark sky, ghosts on silent wings. Barn owls are powerful creatures, their feathers so soft they barely move the air, reminding me that there is strength in softness, power in silence, and that staying soft and quiet does not mean you cannot raise your voice when you so choose.

If you can, go and listen to the owls near where you live. If you can't, then you might take a trip to an owl sanctuary or Falconry, where you can meet and learn about birds of prey including owls, and support their conservation to give back to the avatars of Blodeuwedd in a direct way.

Research online what owls live in your area and what their nature is. What are their feathers like? Are they big or small? What sounds do they make? Are they night owls, or birds of dawn and dusk?

As you learn about the owls near you, they may teach you something deeper. They behaviour and nature of living beings hold magical clues for us.

The cry of the tawny owl reminds me that Blodeuwedd was born from a need to relate, and shaped her life around love and choice. The silence of the barn owl on the hunt reminds me that she had patience and determination in her seeking, and that she did achieve her goals. Though her story reminds us to be careful what we seek for we create our lives within the boundaries of the way the world is.

Weirdly Wyrd

There's another way that Blodeuwedd's tale has always spoken to me, however, one which is woven wider into the systems we live within.

I was always the weird kid at school, the odd one out. I noticed mostly because the others would treat me like I was different somehow, not one of them. I didn't really understand –

weren't we all individuals? Weren't we all different to each other? Slowly I realised that some of us just don't fit in, and that most people I encountered didn't see the world as I did.

The magic, the beauty, the infinite possibilities.

When I heard Blodeuwedd's story I felt a kindred spirit. Here she was, dragged into a world with rules and expectations that must have felt so strange.

We're just going to take a short tangent, but it's relevant, trust me.

It is estimated that between 5-10% of humans have ADHD, which means there are quite a few of us in the world, but we're in the minority and so our modern life is not built to suit us as well as it suits people whose brains are more "typical".

ADHD comes under the social banner "neurodivergent" because our brains are different enough from the "typical" that we struggle with the way the world has been built. There are evolutionary advantages to the neurodivergent traits that become ADHD, autism, dyslexia, and more. For example, as a species we benefit from a small number of our community being impulsive enough to explore and discover new things, being able to think outside the box, being extra focussed on special interests. These are the people who find both danger and new foods, who invent and create new and wonderful technologies, who commune with spirits, and who have strengths in specific ways of thinking and seeing the world. When allowed to work to our strengths we are creative, playful, and powerful problem solvers.

Today, however, in settled communities with dense populations and regimented working expectations – post agricultural development – we're at a disadvantage. And because we run counter to the expected norm we're regularly punished for it, which means that we end up with mental health issues and trauma. Like Blodeuwedd we're out of place and expected to fit in with everyone else.

In nomadic cultures, roaming the land, following the cycles and seasons of our bodies and the sun, ADHD folk have been proven to be healthier, happier, and thriving more than people without the ADHD neurotype.

(A note on nuance: I know, some of you are cross with me because ADHD is a disability. I'm not downplaying the very real challenges that neurodivergent folk can have in today's world, or indeed for those with learning difficulties and such on top, regardless of the culture. It is also true, however, that in a different environment the traits that so often cause problems are strengths, and that so many of us are struggling more than we should be because we've been damaged by expectations, attitudes, and repeated exclusions.)

Back to the story...

It took almost 30 years for me to discover that my brain is actually, neurologically, different to the majority of my peers, and different enough for it to affect my experience of the world, my expression, my behaviour, mannerisms, even way of speaking. They noticed, even if they didn't know why. I was weird, different.

Different enough to warrant a medical diagnosis, it turns out, though I wouldn't swap my brain for the world. Like Blodeuwedd, I did not think like they did. (Unlike Blodeuwedd, I never plotted to murder someone, not even my neglectful husband.)

And like Blodeuwedd, I was a wild, curious spirit crammed into the confines of a world that did not make sense to me, and that I did not make sense to.

Before I knew I was ADHD, I knew I was like Blodeuwedd. No, not a flower spirit made by magicians into a wife, but a natural spirit stuffed into an unnatural life. Throughout my teens I disappeared into books, avoided the violence of the bullies and the catcalls on the street by hiding in libraries and magic circles. There I learned about paganism, about natural magic and spirits, and faeries and land-wights, and when I finally met Blodeuwedd I realized that it was not that I was wrong or broken but that, like her I was just in the wrong place. It was up to me to remember my own nature, and to shape my life to suit me. To remember that I was Wyrd – magical – and not just weird in the insulting way my young peers had meant.

Whether you are neurodivergent or not, as someone drawn to a magical path it is likely that you have found yourself outside of the expectations of society, in small or large ways. Disability, queerness, race, gender, age, and unusual spiritual path, and even just being in a strange place can all put us at odds with the norms or roles we are expected to fulfil in any given moment. For some of us it happens all the time, for many reasons, for others it is occasional or just in one way, but I suspect you, dear magical reader, have experienced being out of place and struggling to conform to rules which do not fit.

It seems like a small thing to see yourself in a thousand-year-old legend, like a strange thing to recognise a kindred spirit in a murderous flower-woman, but for me it was healing. It was healing to hear about a powerful being struggling in the world, who went against expectations and social norms, and who has since become recognised as a goddess with magic and lessons to share.

As Blodeuwedd shifts her shape through her story, this metamorphosis continued in the years since, when modern pagans heard her call and lifted her up as deity. I hope that the recognition she receives now has gone some way to healing the spirit that she was, and it feels to me like she has become so much bigger than a merely wicked woman as she is sometimes described.

Like this goddess, we shift our shapes, and are often forced to take roles in life that do not fit us well. We can learn, however, to choose which shapes we take when, which masks we wear because they make life easier, and when we put them down. By exploring shapeshifting as a magical and energetic act we can learn from Blodeuwedd to recognise which aspect is the true us underlying the faces and forms, which makes it easier to come home to ourselves, however often we have to play the game of "acceptability".

Exercise – Many Shapes, One Heart

In a time and space you won't be disturbed, with space to move if you can, get comfortable. Read through the steps below and consider how you'd like to approach the process.

Invite Blodeuwedd to guide you if she will. You might make an offering at your altar, something you can take out and give to the plants later. You get to choose how to approach this goddess, the keys are to approach with respect, and to release entitlement. She, in turn, gets to choose whether she works with you. Focus on gratitude rather than expectations, and let the experience unfold.

If you have a drum or a rattle you might like to start a steady rhythm and let the sound carry you. If you don't, you can chant her name softly to yourself, clap a heartbeat, use a recorded ambient music or drumbeat for journeying, or just rest in silence. Rhythm or music of some kind is useful for many people in staying present for this kind of work, and it helps to gently create trance, which you'll be using here.

Notice your body resting on the earth. Allow your breathing to become steady and feel yourself as a physical being. Slowly let your awareness expand to take in your emotional self, your feelings. Next, let it expand to your thoughts, your mental self. However you feel, whatever you think, it's all welcome here.

When you're ready, let your awareness expand to your energetic self, your spirit.

You don't need to know what this means, just let yourself feel into it. If you want to, imagine your different selves like nesting dolls, your physical body inside your emotional body, inside your mental body, inside your energetic body.

Breathe into your energetic self and begin to imagine it expanding out, like you are made of flowers and plants, growing on the earth.

Spend some time exploring this. How does it feel? Smell? Taste? What are your thoughts like? You might feel like moving as flowers, and you can choose to explore this too.

When you're ready, breathe in, and as you breathe out relax and release this experience, feeling yourself coming back to your human form.

Notice how this feels.

Finally, breathe into your energetic self again and imagine yourself becoming an owl or other animal or bird.

What does this feel like? What do you notice? Hear? Smell? Taste? How do you want to move, if at all?

Take your time.

And when you feel it is time, breathe in, like you are gathering up all the experiences you have had, and breathe out, letting them settle into your self as you release this shape and come back to the human you, and stop whichever rhythm or music you were using to keep present, if any.

Wiggle your fingers and toes, pat yourself down, say your name three times, notice your skin, your tongue in your mouth, your butt on the floor... Remind yourself of your human shape.

Give yourself a moment to remember the different experiences and notice: what was the same through all of them? What part of you remained the same, regardless of what shape you chose? What is the heart of you? Learning how to recognise this is a powerful step in being whole and finding your path through all the expectations and situations life throws at you.

Thank Blodeuwedd in your own way.

Make any notes you would like to remember, and ground yourself back into being human by doing something mundane like hoovering, or washing the dishes. Eating something salty and crunchy is good here too.

You can return to this again, adapt it how you choose, and use it to explore how different shapes feel, and who you are underneath all the masks and roles you might take on in your life.

An Outline of the Steps

1. Get comfortable, choose music, silence, or an instrument.
2. Invite Blodeuwedd to guide you. Make an offering.
3. Connect to the earth, become aware of your whole self – physical, emotional, mental, and energetic.
4. Imagine becoming flowers – explore this.
5. Remember being human – notice how this feels.
6. Imagine becoming an owl – explore this.
7. Return to how you began – reflect on the thread of you that was present throughout.
8. Thank Blodeuwedd.
9. Make notes.
10. Get grounded!

The Wild World

Let us take a moment to expand our vision a little further. I've shared with you a little of my story relating to situations that an individual might find themselves in, and then, more broadly, ways in which society is often shaped in ways that leave us out of place and forgetting ourselves as we play the roles expected of us.

Now, let us turn for a moment and reflect on Blodeuwedd as avatar of the natural world. We Western humans tend to think of ourselves as separate, but her story shows a continuum between plant and human and animal. A kinship of life on earth. By listening to the flowers and learning lessons from the owls, and then exploring the experience of borrowing their shapes, perhaps this has given you an inkling of the deeper wisdom of Blodeuwedd.

We are part of the web that she exists throughout, interconnected and related to all of life. When you explore life from these many perspectives, notice what you learn about the nature of other beings. Of animism – where all beings have spirits and are alive, in relationship with each other – and of what that might mean for how we can approach living in the wider world, as part of nature rather than thinking of ourselves as apart from it all.

I invite you to reflect on Blodeuwedd as a Goddess that lives in all forms of life. If she is present throughout that web, then how might you honour her in your approach to other-than-human nature?

The Magicians, Gwydion and Math, took the flowers without asking and shaped them for their ends. In many ways her story is a reminder that it does not end well when we act in entitled ways, imposing our will on the natural world with no thought for its nature and needs.

And Blodeuwedd reminds us that when the world does that to us, we can push back.

When we remember our own truth, our own power, and our place as part of the living world, we remember that we can live in relation with nature. We share our magic and power with the world, and the systems that harm the environment harm us too, because they treat us in the same way. Many of us have internalised this, and cannot entirely escape it, but we can listen, begin to shapeshift ourselves and remember our kinship.

By rooting, dancing, and flying with Blodeuwedd, perhaps we can remember that we are all nature, and in that connection, we can work together to heal. By treating ourselves kindly, by being with others authentically, and by being with the rest of the natural world as family, we become free in our interconnectedness.

When we remember that we are already whole, and hold our wild, soft, hearts tenderly open with fierce truth of who we are, then we move into that dance of life with the flowers, and the owls, and the beauty of following what we love into truth.

Under the Serpent Glare

Sian Sibley

Don't you look at me, he screamed.
As he hit her
Because she wore no veil
Look at the floor he yelled
As he raped her
Her skirt was too short
Look away bitch he screamed
As his fist slams home
You are no daughter of mine
Submit
Give in
Give up
I own you; you are mine
You are my toy

And in her mind
Deep down in the dark place
Where the forgotten Goddess lives
She hears the Hiss
The sound of scales
The eyes ablaze
And she hears a voice, a whisper rising
Look Up My daughter
Raise your eyes
Make him face your rage
Show him your power
For you are not his, you are MINE!!
And I will make him stone.

The creation of Medusa, the snake-headed gorgon, is a myth that screams of the patriarchy, not just the rape itself but the punishment of the human woman for her rape by a god, displays a need for total violation, of body, of will and of spirit.

Medusa was one of the Gorgon sisters; the other sisters were Stheno and Euryale. Both sisters were immortal and already snake-haired, whereas Medusa, although snake-haired, was mortal. In Ovid's Metamorphosis, she is described as a priestess in the temple of Athena. Poseidon, obsessed with Medusa's beauty and virginity, rapes her within the temple. Athena, a virgin Goddess, sees the rape as Medusa's fault because she is too beautiful and transforms her into a snake-headed monster whose gaze turns all who look her in the eye to stone.

In condemning Medusa to this fate, Athena, in my opinion, shows herself as a male version of what a woman should be. Projected from the forehead of Zeus in the act of male parthenogenesis, an act that is completely against nature.

Athena has no female energy and comes with all the correspondences of a male. The martial nature is shown by the spear, helmet and shield. The jealous heart, she is jealous of Medusa's beauty which was said to rival her own, and the condemnation of a woman for their own rape is a very male concept. Think about how it is said today, "She was begging for it", and "She deserved it"; these are common themes in victim-blaming culture and are familiar to male society and, sadly, to the women who fall beneath that patriarchal bias.

The snake in myth and legend has long been associated with wisdom, from the Ouroboros, the symbol of the continuation of existence, to Asclepius and Hermes snake staffs, denoting medicine and science. The use of snake imagery in the bible, the changing of Moses' staff into a snake and the giving of free will in the Garden of Eden are also symbols of the transmission of magical and transgressive thought. The Snake goddesses of Knossos and the Cobra-Headed goddesses of Egypt were all-wise and all-knowing and honoured as world creatrixes. When the more patriarchal divinities came into ascendency, they made demons of the goddesses before them, creating mythologies around their vile and evil ways to discourage millennia-old religious practices. When you look at the mythology surrounding Medusa, a tremendous amount of material can be useful in ritual and magical practice, particularly for empowering women who have undergone a traumatic experience.

In analysing the myth, we can construct ritual to support a woman who needs to reestablish herself after trauma. Taking a feminist interpretation of the Medusa myth, we can reframe the story and disrupt the victim-blaming narrative surrounding her character. Rather than holding Medusa responsible for her assault, these interpretations frame her as a survivor who endured a traumatic experience, a goddess who is powerful because of the trauma she has experienced and not despite that trauma.

When we look at Medusa's powers, the first is that of her Gaze; Medusa literally can turn those who would attack her to stone. The female gaze is something that men fear greatly, and for millennia, women have been forced into an attitude of acquiescence to their men. You only have to look at the artwork showing the Virgin Mary below.

The gaze of the virgin is perpetually down to the floor or, alternatively, up to the sky. She is very rarely shown with her eyes forward. She is the mother of God and yet is shown in an attitude of subservience to all who look upon her. The message to women is clear: you must bow down; you are less than, we are above you, and you cannot be our equal.

Medusa imagery, on the other hand, shows her looking straight on. She is reminiscent of those confrontational goddesses such as Kali.

She is showing her power here; her gaze challenges and defies.

Sigmund Freud and other psychologists equate the decapitation of Medusa with the Castration of Kronos. Looking at the picture, you can see why the Greeks thought that the head of Medusa looked like the Vagina, with the nose being the Clitoris, the mouth being the vaginal entrance, and the wild hair being the Vulva. It represents female reproductive power, which is uncontrolled and dangerous. The paper "The Laugh of Medusa" describes it like this. "Men say there are two unrepresentable things: death and the feminine sex. That's because they need femininity to be associated with death; the jitters give them a hard-on! for themselves! They need to be afraid of us. Look at the trembling Perseus's moving backwards toward us, clad in apostrophes."

Stories and myths about the Evil Eye are found worldwide, and women are most commonly accused of delivering or being the victim of this evil eye. One cure for the evil eye is a serpent stone, which is the crystalised leavings of the mating of serpents left behind after reproduction. It is ironic that Medusa, who has the ultimate "Evil Eye" is possessed of the very snakes that are seen to be its cure.

Her gaze has a massive power; this forward-looking, direct confrontation with the female energy is too much to take and causes the man to become stone.

This is another female power as we are the creators of form, the ultimate energy restriction into space and time. We embody the soul so that life can exist on the planes of form. In turning her enemies to stone, Medusa encases them in so much structure that she causes them to become inert and unable to hurt her anymore. She silences them with only her gaze. Men fear the female's removal of their primal male energy and cannot cope when a woman looks at them in the eye.

Remember, in patriarchal religions, form is seen as evil; it results from the fall from heaven, which is outside the reality of mortal forms. It is the removal from God, who is seen as solely male. Heaven is seen as separate from nature, and the natural world, which is seen as female, women are seen as degraded and less than those male intellectuals who exist closer to the mind of God. The idea of being immersed in the physicality of the natural world is too much for the male ego to bear, to be in the control of a mere woman, to acknowledge that you come from her; this is anathema to the patriarchy. This is why the rule of female reproduction is most important to the male evangelical Christian. The power to make life, to bring form and beauty into the world is not a male power but a female one.

Medusa can only be seen by Perseus in reflection. He sees her in reverse; she is evil and powerless to him, and he can decapitate her. In reality, she is the power of the universe; as such, in the same way, that the God of the Torah is seen, can never be seen face-on.

The reflection of Medusa takes us into the realm of the Moon, where all imagination takes form. Where the receptive power of the female ensouls the body and creates the universe of reality. It is the place of the dead, the otherworld, and the female is strong here. In the liminality between the real and the reflected, the teacher goddesses live, Hekate and Ereshkigal, Innana, as she descends into form.

Perseus cuts off Medusa's head with a sickle, not a sword. The sickle symbolises Time and Saturn, the ultimate mother of form. Joseph Campbell speaks about the death of Medusa, saying "The legend of Perseus beheading Medusa means, specifically, that "the Hellenes overran the goddess's chief shrines" and "stripped her priestesses of their Gorgon masks", the latter being apotropaic faces worn to frighten away the profane. That is to say, there occurred in the early thirteenth century B.C. an actual historical rupture, a sort of sociological trauma, which has been registered in this myth".

Even after her decapitation, Medusa still exercises her power of creation. As her head is cut from her body, she gives birth to the winged horse Pegasus and the Giant Chrysaor. Her head is placed into the Shield of Pallas Athena and is used to turn Perseus into the heroic figure he is remembered as today.

So, at the end of the myth, we have the death of the creative Goddess, the removal of her head and its use as a weapon by a man. In reality, we have control of women's sex by a man wielding a weapon of war. A man who is too scared of her power to look her in the eye while he violently causes her death, her sex is then used as a weapon to control others.

Medusa in Magic and Ritual

Approaching Medusa in ritual must be done with the utmost respect and care. She is a goddess who has been defiled and would be an ideal goddess to approach if you are the victim of trauma of any kind but particularly trauma involving rape or sexual assault.

I have found when working with victims of sexual assault that women are taught to feel responsible for their own assault. They will self-blame to justify why this thing has happened to them. A rape or sexual assault is a heinous act; they cannot fathom why someone would do that to them. Therefore, rather than allowing anger, sadness, loss and trauma to be expressed, they push the trauma down behind the pseudo-protection of guilt that they must have done something to deserve this terrible punishment.

We do it all the time. We are taught from childhood not to be angry when something is done to us. It is not feminine to be angry, or as Donald Trump, a famous sexual assaulter, would put it, to be a nasty woman. In school, girls are often told that the boy who has hit or pulled their hair probably fancies them and does not know how to express those feelings. Women are advised to carry rape whistles in college; this gives the idea that should they be raped and being without their rape whistle, they didn't call for help, so it's their fault.

Women are taught that men have no control over their sexual urges and it is a woman's responsibility to avoid tempting the man if she does so? Well, she deserves what she gets. You only have to look at what is happening in Iran now to understand why we must stand together with our sisters in other societies to resist this non-sensical way of thinking.

Women in society do not have the power to say no to a man who is looking for sex. Look at the incel ideologies, to know what type of world these men want to have. They are Perseus coming at us with their shield reversed, and I say we meet them head-on and turn them to stone.

The following ritual and meditation are my gift to you to reclaim your power with the aid of the Great Snake-headed Goddess Medusa.

A Ritual of Reclaiming Your Own Medusa

A reclaiming ritual involving Medusa for a woman who has been sexually assaulted can be a powerful way to draw strength from the Gorgon Medusa, often seen as a symbol of a raped woman, a survivor and a powerful Goddess who has reclaimed her reproductive and sexual power.

Please be aware that this ritual should be approached with sensitivity and the consent and comfort of the survivor. There needs to be a true sisterhood here with support and love to allow the woman to accept what has happened, express her anger, trauma and sadness at her experience and grieve for the person she was before the assault.

It is a private and safe space; no men should be allowed in this ritual space. Should the woman want her husband or partner to be a comfort, he should be nearby but not allowed into the ritual. Work may need to be done for the partner of a rape victim to enable him or her to come to terms with what has been done to their loved one.

Materials Needed:

It is a private and safe space; no men should be allowed in this ritual space. Should the woman want her husband or partner to be a comfort, he should be nearby but not allowed into the ritual. Work may need to be done for the partner of a rape victim to enable him or her to come to terms with what has been done to their loved one.

A statue or image of Medusa (or a representation of her in art or jewellery).

A mirror.

Candles (black or purple for transformation and healing).

An incense containing Dragon's blood, snakeskin, copal and Mugwort.

Steps:

- Preparation: Find a quiet, safe space where you won't be disturbed. Set up your altar with the image or representation of Medusa, the candles, and any cleansing herbs. Create a serene atmosphere with soft music or calming sounds if desired.

- Grounding and Centering: Sit comfortably before your altar, close your eyes, and take several deep breaths to centre yourself. Visualise roots extending from your body into the Earth, grounding you in safety and strength.
- Invoke your main deity. For me, this would be Hekate; this is a wonderful Goddess to invoke in this situation, as Hekate was the Goddess that helped Demeter and Persephone after Hades took her to the underworld.

My invocation to Hekate follows, but please feel free to use one of your own to Hekate or another Goddess you are following.

A Call to Hekate

Mother of the form around us
Life and death in one deep breath
Universal hearts compassion
Mother both from birth to death
Cup and womb of power indwelling
Give to me the kingdom's key
Shadow to the Light's great power
Mother of the world to be
Scythed one standing at the crossroads
In between the dark and light
Give to us the ancient power
Grant to us the ancient sight

Invocation of Medusa

Snake headed
Serpent scaled
Mighty one
Defiled one
Reviled one
Goddess of the serpent gaze

Defender of women
You who hold the power of creation
Energy's Anchor
Who binds men to the stone
Old one
Hekate's serpentine servant
Come and aid your daughter
In the names of Hekate, Ereshkigal, Neboutosaleth
I call to you
Come and aid us
In our Rage

- Candle: Light the candles and focus on the image of Medusa. As you do, breathe deeply and imagine Medusa's fierce and protective energy enveloping you. See yourself surrounded by her strength.

- Mirror Gazing: one of the women needs to hold the mirror in front of the woman's face. The woman must look directly at herself, deep into her own eyes. One woman should stand behind her so that she can see her face in the mirror. This woman will be the embodiment of Medusa. When the ritual conversation begins, she must look directly into the eyes of Medusa.

- There needs to be a conversation between the embodied Medusa and the victim of assault. This will be the Goddess guiding the woman to the realisation that she did not cause her own rape; nothing she could have done would have given the man the right to do this to her. Pointing out that she has the right to be angry and getting her to express her anger by screaming, crying or hitting something (sometimes, this can be very distressing for the woman supporting her). Once during a ritual of this type, the woman believed sincerely that she should have been able to fight off the man and that if she had tried harder, the rape would not have happened. I am a 4ft 11 female, and I held her down on the floor until she realised she could never have fought off a man of 6ft. That allowed her to release her guilt and cry for the first time since her attack; she screamed and cursed at me while I did this, which was very hard for me to do. I needed support from the women in the circle after this. But it helped her, and it was a price I was willing to pay to help my beloved friend. So, be aware of this type of ritual's impact on the women in the circle.

- Turning to Stone – After the cathartic release and acceptance of what has happened, there needs to be some sort of acknowledgement that while this was an awful thing to have happened to the woman, she will go forward with the memory of the assault and the understanding that it will never leave her but that she has the strength to live her life with love and honour not letting the experience colour who she is. I usually do this by allowing her to smash something representing the man turned to stone. It can be a statue of a male or maybe even just a vase or cup, but it must be something ceramic that will smash on the floor.

Once ready, she must voice her release of the man's hold over her. Something like;

Man (you can use the name if she knows it) I am scarred,
I am hurt,
you think you took my body and soul,
that you possess me and the life before me
but I say now before the eyes of Medusa that you have no
    power over me.
My soul burns with the power of the moon, the Goddess
    walks within me,

I am not defiled.
It is you who are reviled.
I Gaze into your eyes, and I see you, man.
I see your quest for power.
I see your weak heart and spirit.
Your meanness and depravity
and I make you stone.
You may not hurt me
you may not tie me down
you may not despoil me
for I am glorious, and I walk in the Light of the serpent-
    haired queen.

She smashes the statue.

Move the mirror down between the woman's legs. Let her
see the Medusa within.

Let her see that this man has not destroyed her sex; it
is hers and hers alone to give in passion and love, and it
is not a weapon to be used against her. It is a joy for her
to share

She is still whole; even after this, her own decapitation,
Medusa still holds her power.

- The speaking – allow all women to speak their truth.
  Expressions of love and support, sharing common
  experiences if they have them, when did they first feel
  male rage against them, show the woman that they care
  for her deeply and always will.
- Closing and Gratitude: Close the ritual with your own
  usual dismissal, thanking Hekate and Medusa for their
  strength, guidance, and protection. Blow out the candles
  and extinguish any cleansing herbs if used.

- Continued Support: Healing is an ongoing process, and seeking professional support from therapists, counsellors, or support groups is essential for your journey.

Meditation with Medusa

She rises in front of me, sibilant and sensuous.

The sound of the hissing rises from the darkness around me.

She is turned away, and I wonder if this is a good idea. I am fearful that I am not enough.

She turns.

Her eyes are old. They shine with the creation of universes.

She is the foundation of form, standing with her mouth agape and eyes flaring open. Labian serpents writhing in passion around her. No man can look at her, emasculated by her strength, he becomes stone, inert and passionless. But I can look upon her beautiful face; I, too, am a woman, a reflection of her power in the world. No more hiding, no more guilt I scream with joy at her gaze. An orgasm of acceptance of my power.

Deep inside, I feel the warmth descend, the ache within pulsing with a rhythm as old as creation itself. My own medusa throbbing, remembering the feel of passion and joy. Remembering Her. She is the power of my sex and the slow, honeyed drip of my desire.

She gives me power over myself, not to be removed by any man or cursed by any woman blind to the power she has given away.

She is my creative urge, drive to make, and imagination-given form.

How dare they try to control me? How dare they think my being is theirs to own, abuse, defile. She gives me words to share:

She sits behind my eyes and watches
Inside my womb, she rises
Shining like a serpent, glorious
She rides on the currents of the wind
She faces the anger of the Earth
She rides despair like a tempering sword
She is the mother of the glorious women
The unfettered manes of hair, snake-like and boundless
The eyes on fire
The wild dance
The inescapable vice of control, unaccepted
Who are you to tell me who I am
When in me beats the heart of the serpent-headed queen
Who are you to judge me in your stagnant mediocrity
Your blind acceptance of the yoke of man.
You are no sister to me
I rise, towering, my breast ablaze with passion
I run with the demons and with the damned
I fly with the Angelos singing with her voice
I am Medusa's child, my gaze destroys
Now come Brother, tell me again how I should be in the
    world?

The Romance of Mis and Dubh Ruis
A Template for Navigating Grief and Trauma

Victoria Scobie

The Romance of Mis and Dubh Ruis comes from Irish Mythology and was documented in the 17th century – though largely forgotten until manuscripts, that included this tale, were rediscovered in the 1950s. Before I detail the story itself, I will give some context as to how I discovered Mis, and the imprint her story has left on me as part of my own healing journey.

As someone who loves reading and learning new things, I turned to mythology during the collective trauma that was the COVID-19 pandemic. After long shifts navigating ways of working that changed day to day to respond to the crisis, I sought total escapism from what was the reality of working within the healthcare system at that time. It began with reading about the Greek Myths in my spare time – the various Gods and Goddesses and their dramatic stories. They were entertaining up to a point, and there were some moral lessons to be found, but what really caught my imagination was the modern re-telling of these stories with the women at the centre. After centuries of censorship, being demoted to a few lines in a poem or portrayed as a depthless monster – suddenly I could hear the voices of Medusa, Circe and Penelope – to name a few. How they approached difficulties, that any modern woman may have, by being responsive to what life threw at them and utilising their emotions, intellect and experience.

Next, my interests moved to Norse mythology, then closer to home with the Welsh tales from the *Mabinogion* and Celtic Myths about the Cailleach and Fionn mac Cumhaill. Behind the predominant heroic tales of Gods, Knights, Kings, special sons and quests you could find glimpses of the divine female and her role. Often passive but wise, maternal but grieving, maiden-like in ethereal naivety – nevertheless 'real' women could be found in these stories. So, these stories were the backdrop to my pandemic experience where every day I observed the spectrum of responses to trauma. Patients varied widely in their responses: from stoicism, gallows humour and stiff upper lip "keep calm and carry on" to hysteria, anger, sulkiness and full-blown rage.

The notion that I was finding escapism in these myths was, of course, an illusion, as many of them deal with themes such as grief, trauma, loss and navigating uncertainty. What was creeping up on me was my own trauma which I had bottled away for the time being as a survival strategy. Four years prior to the pandemic I had lost my son, Daniel – he was stillborn – and with his loss, my vision of the future disintegrated. In a frenzy of action, I had packed up my life in New Zealand and returned to source – my family in Scotland – to hibernate and work out how to put myself back together again. I had tried the mainstream options – counselling, self-help books, a new job, a new location but that wasn't enough. Learning about Mis was one of many pieces of the jigsaw puzzle which helped. I hope her story resonates with you and any loss you have experienced. Looking back, I now see loss as a divine wound, and the story offers up some treasure as to how we may approach our own losses. At a time when I was immersed in Arthurian legends and Greek warrior heroes – Mis and Dubh Ruis really stand out as a couple who found another way to approach challenges.

The following version is adapted from Jennifer Heath's telling from *On the Edge of Dream: The Women of Celtic Myth and Legend* (1998). It mentions a Gaelic word, caoineadh which means a eulogy or lament sung at wakes and funerals.

Mis stumbled onto the battlefield. Daire Mor's head and golden torc had been taken for trophy. She knew him by his knuckles – that had tickled her ears when she sat beside him on the King's seat. At night he had covered her with calfskins while her mother sang. When Mis's mother died, Daire Mor wept openly and wailed caoineadh like a woman.

The residue of his smile was a notched scarlet slash on his empty shoulders. Mis caught his streaming blood in cupped palms and drank. Sucked his wounds. Licked his bruises. She could not keen, she could not sing caoineadh. After many days she stood. Hair clotted with blood, guts, marrow and dirt.

She forgot her father, her people, her home, her language. Speechless, thoughtless, without memory. Hair sprouted over Mis's body, raging appetite pulled at her skinny belly. She scented and stalked, beast, bird and man. She rushed swift as wind, outraced pain. Mis caught every bird, every man who ventured onto her mountain. Her long nails toughened into talons. She ripped and shredded. Killing gave form to her grief and fury. Bones piled high on Mis's mountain.

They named that deserted country Clanmaurice and the King of Munster issued a proclamation that Mis should not be killed, for he was curious to see the wild maiden, who ravished all life that came near her. He promised a great reward together with the settlement and rent of Clanmaurice to whoever could bring her into custody alive. And many worthy warriors tried, but Mis devoured them all. One day music shook the desolation of Mis's mountain. Melody borne by breezes, reflected on tickling water. Woven round with a human voice, like strong, spiralling silver. The notes encased her. Scratched at Mis's heart.

The source was a young man sitting cross-legged playing a harp. Dubh Ruis, the King's harper had asked for gold as part of his plan to rescue the wild maiden.

Mis burst at the trespasser. He did not move. Did not look up. Dainty knuckles. Eloquent fingers. He stroked his harp with a loving, soothing hand. A glint caught her eye – yellow nuggets arranged on a blue silk cloak. The gold coins, the colour of her father's beard and of his regal torc, gold like his polished chariot, like her mother's rings and bracelets.

Dubh Ruis played on, Mis wobbled with curiosity. She touched the gold again. He plucked a note. He smiled at Mis. Shy, beardless, fearless, girlish, smile. He moved closer to her, hand on her knee. She flinched. Backed away. He inched closer. Dubh Ruis set down his harp. He parted the heavy wall of Mis's hair. And carefully and gently he made love to her.

Afterwards Mis was famished and leaped around her mountain hunting and killing a stag for them to eat. Dubh Ruis stopped her from devouring the meat raw. He had prepared a cooking pit where a cauldron of water boiled on the fire. He skinned and butchered the animal, singing a hymn of thanks to the stag. As the stew simmered the harper sang songs of her clan, of Daire Mor, of heroes' deeds and all her people's sires.

Dubh Ruis served Mis the meal she had caught and he had cooked. With flatbreads he had brought, Mis copied the actions of scooping the stew up with the bread. When they were done, Dubh Ruis took Mis's hand and guided her to the bubbling cauldron. He bathed her in the warm water. Strand by strand, bits of her thatched hair shed. Her rawness began to wash away. Dubh Ruis prepared a bed. He cradled Mis. Rocked her the night long.

Dubh Ruis stayed with Mis at the foot of her mountain for many months and she did not leap away. Now he loved her. Day by day, he cared for her. Taught her to rest. To coax tunes from his harp. He carried her away from the terrifying war cries with lovely harmonies. He taught her to hunt with weapons and ask permission and give thanks to the animals.

And Mis was calmed by his patience. Mesmerized by friendship she had not known since Daire Mor's death. Over those months, handful by handful each day, the hair that smothered, concealed and swaddled her fell to the ground. When at last Dubh Ruis cut Mis's talons and threw them in the fire, Mis neither fought nor squirmed but acquiesced, trusting as a baby.

That night Mis dreamed of Daire Mor. Restored and happy in death, her father embraced her, kissed her cheek and bid her farewell. Mis woke keening. She wept and clapped and screamed. Her first clear words spoken – a caoineadh for Daire Mor – stormed out of her mouth. With this the last of her long, thick pelt disappeared. A handsome young woman emerged.

Dubh Ruis consoled Mis. He washed the tears from her cheeks. He brushed and plaited her smooth brown hair and dressed her in his cloak. Dubh Ruis took Mis from the mountain, over the plain where battle had been done and Autumn flowers now bloomed. He presented her to the King of Munster and Mis met the King proudly, eye to eye, as the daughter of a chieftain come to take her own high seat.

The King gave Dubh Ruis the promised treasure together with the settlement and rent of Clanmaurice. Dubh Ruis and Mis married. She had four children and yearly honoured her father's name. She stayed with Dubh Ruis forever until he died.

Then Mis called forth the other women. She took off her shoes and her jewels and loosened her hair. She dressed his body. She laid him out upon her table. She keened for him a caoineadh, verses beautiful and breathless. Music so magical it leaped three times from her mouth across the threshold between the living and the dead, and there contained and kept in readiness the story of their passion.

Such a powerful, moving story; it offers more depth of understanding of grief than most of what we have to offer within the modern health service. With Mis the closeness to her father is obvious as she recalls his attention and care. The playfulness of the knuckles that "tickled her ears" and his ability to show vulnerability in front of his daughter in his "wailing" for his wife who died. We are aware of this backdrop of a secure father figure and respected leader in touch with both the masculine and feminine elements of his personality. The violent death and

Mis's view of her beheaded father on the battle fields leads to a break in identity. Her source of security forcibly removed, she must embody the disrupted masculine elements to stay safe – the talons and violence form a solid fortress – separating her from her community. She becomes monstrous. With such defences the "worthy warriors" have no chance. You can imagine them active and forward moving on their steads, wishing to capture and contain her, efficiently and swiftly. But this is the wrong approach.

So, I invite you to think of your own losses in context to Mis and her extreme transformation. It may be a bereavement, the loss of a friendship or end of a relationship or even the loss of home as you move to a new area or new job. When your security was removed, did Mis rise up in you? How were you monstrous? How did you build your fortress to keep people away? Did you develop teeth and talons – more jagged edges when interacting with others? And something I've noticed with many of my patients – when strong emotions are repressed how does it come out in your body? For Mis the inability to grieve and wail like her father did, means this energy turns inward, leading to her monstrous transformation into a vicious animal.

There is strong evidence in medicine for repressed emotions feeding physical symptoms and illnesses. Diabetes worsens as blood sugar levels increase along with our stress response. People with asthma or COPD (chronic obstructive lung disease) have more flare ups when under long term stress and repressed emotions feed skin conditions such as eczema and psoriasis. Plus, significant mental illnesses can often be traced back to previous trauma which has been repressed or not properly processed. The degree of impact depends on how old the trauma is – in particular, if it occurred at the pre-verbal stage (from birth to 3 years old) – and how severe or sustained the trauma was. This is well documented with the Adverse Childhood Experiences (ACEs) research which shows how childhood adversity can be linked to physical health issues in adult life. With a modern trauma-informed lens, Mis is less of a monster and looks more like a massively traumatized young woman.

So, with this in mind, what are the pearls of healing from Dubh Ruis and how can we use these to guide us through grief and loss. Dubh Ruis is notable less macho than the warriors previously described. He has a "shy, beardless, fearless girlish smile" and "dainty fingers". His approach is in stark contrast to the galloping warriors – he is tentative, meandering and opens with music. I imagine him spiraling the forest around Mis, playing his harp, getting slightly close and closer with each loop. He settled himself in the forest and waits until she approaches him. He spends months in the forest with her, gently building trust and eventually their love connection. Dubh Ruis cares for her body, mind and spirit and over time she comes back to herself. Pulling out elements of Dubh Ruis' approach I invite you to consider this template if you have suffered a loss or are supporting someone moving through a period of loss. These steps merely offer guidance and ideas and I recommend trying the ones that most interest you.

Step 1 – Gentle Approach: consider a more passive approach – for those grieving this may mean attending family get togethers or meeting a friend for coffee but not being able to fully engage as you did before your grief. With those that you trust it is ok to be authentic rather than "putting a face on it" and they will understand why you may need to be silent at this time. Simply being around other people you trust is helpful. Don't force discussion with the bereaved about the loss if it is not welcomed. There is often an impression that talking it out, going through a loss or trauma and externalising how one feels can fast track the grief process. I have not found this to be the case. People will talk when they are ready, and it may be with a stranger or a therapist rather than a close friend or family member.

Journalling or making art may be easier than speaking about things aloud. Also, people often open up more when positioned side by side rather than a more confronting face to face position. So, think about invites out for a walk, to the movies or to watch sports.

Step 2 – Calming the Nervous System – for Dubh Ruis he used music to soothe and intrigue Mis. Thinking more widely, consider what soothes your nervous system – when you feel tense and like a wound-up coil- what helps the coil unwind and release. The nervous system is not just the brain but all of the nerves supplying our whole body and tying into our emotions and feelings. Music is a great place to start -listen to music in the car, at home, with your earphones when out for a walk or doing chores. Think about your perfect playlist – what songs may you feel calm, sleepy, excited, sorrowful, pensive – and match the playlist to what you need. Are there songs from your childhood or teenage years that take you back to happy memories and carefree times? – tap into that. Sound therapy is a great source of healing dating back to ancient times and is often overlooked. It is only when the nervous system is calmed that trauma or loss can be processed – if Mis remained in her agitated, feral state she may still be roaming about the forest. Healing and repair can only occur when we are out of the 'fight or flight' mode and in a rested state.

Step 3 – Body Work – Dubh Ruis bathed Mis in warm water and made love to her, he cut back her hair and sharp talons. He retaught her how to cook meat, enjoy a meal together and by the end of their time together she emerged as an embodied woman ready for marriage and childbearing. Body work is something I find is often overlooked as people approach grief and loss. My patients are often happy to see a counsellor, talk about their response to the loss and discuss about how they could move on from this and rebuild themselves. But bodily responses may hold you back and stop you from moving forward.

Dr Gabor Mate, a retired GP, author and famous healer writes about how traumatic memories are stored in the body and can present years later as physical symptoms. No matter how convincingly we can tell ourselves we are over something and have moved on, our body often sends opposing messages. For myself grief led to social withdrawal and dismissal of self-care – I didn't care what I looked like, what I wore. Hair and makeup lost their importance and I was not eating well as nourishing my body felt pointless. Like Mis – something as simple as bathing can make a huge difference and can feel like a big step in the depths of grief. The act of washing your own skin is a recognition of your body as an important part of you, requiring touch and care. Dressing carefully, paying attention to hair, nails and so on is not selfish it is a reminder of the vessel our spirit resides in. Next steps may include nourishing our body with a home cooked meal and then thinking about movement. Anything from a brief walk around the block, some stretches whilst you sit on the couch, up to a yoga class or going to the gym helps us get back into our body. This movement and caring for our body aids trauma processing – but avoid doing it in a punishing way or comparing yourself to others and their progress. There are specific somatic exercises you can do for emotional release e.g. hip opening exercises and I highly recommend these. Remembering Dubh Ruis rocking Mis to sleep – you will find even rocking your hips side to side lying in bed is soothing and calming for our nervous system – try it! Also, breath work is excellent – I often felt I was unconsciously taking shallow, quick breaths when I was grieving and slowing down the breath brings you back to the present and the movement of your chest. I recommend experimenting with body work – try things that intrigue you and experiment with techniques that you like and what works for you as an individual.

Step 4 – Social Connectedness – this may be relevant further along the grief process when one has moved out of 'hibernation mode'. Dubh Ruis sang songs of Mis's clan, their great achievements and exploits and brought her up to date with all that had happened since she left. Thus, creating a link to people and places from her past – and happy memories prior to her father's death. After my bereavement, returning to Scotland and my family felt like an automatic response. Landscapes and buildings I recognised were very reassuring and seeing family or friends I hadn't seen for years was therapeutic. For example, hearing how someone I went to school with was getting on, who had moved away, who was married or having kids. It was another piece of the puzzle reminding me of my identity within a family and within a community. What could this look like for you? Visiting places from your past, calling a distant cousin for a catch up or reaching out to an old school friend online? This can also mean new social connections – joining groups or clubs where you live or speaking to someone at work you don't know so well. Some processing of grief can be done alone and in isolation but, you can only get so far, then the remaining healing occurs in community. So be sure to choose your community carefully.

Step 5 – Creative Expression / Play – Creative expression is one way to get out of the misery and stagnant energy associated with grief and loss, it can take us out of cyclical pessimistic thought patterns and remind us who we are. Mis learns to play the harp and eventually finds her voice. As her relationship with Dubh Ruis develops they can be playful and enjoy each other. And this, of course, ties back to her positive memories of play with her father and her mother singing her to sleep. Together they are reprocessing trauma memories and embedding more positive memories about both her parents.

Think about the last time you were playful? It's something many adults forget about. It's helpful if you have young children or pets around as playfulness comes so naturally to them- it's just a case of copying and joining in. If not, think about how you played as a child – could you tap into that feeling again? For creativity – do you want to make a mess with paints, sing out of tune around the house, build a sandcastle, write in your journal or do a sport that you love. Make more time for this, enjoy the feeling of freedom in your mind and body and if you're really lucky you may experience what Csikszentmihalyi (2008) calls the 'state of flow'. Experiencing flow is accompanied with sense of accomplishment, meaningfulness and positive mood states. We all know that being creative makes us feel good but now neuroscience can back this up. MRI scans of people in a state of flow have shown increased activity in our dopamine centres – the happy hormone – and less activity to the areas of our brain associated with worry, ruminating and negative mindset. So, creativity is vital to recovery – find your outlet and carve out regular time for it.

Step 6 – Giving back, helping others – all the careful attention and care Dubh Ruis gave to Mis meant she was able to let her guard down, be vulnerable and create an intimate relationship with her lover. Their union is balanced, reciprocal and authentic – a truly divine union. By the end of the story Mis has shed layers of herself – she is no longer the young naïve daughter of a warrior. She leaves the safety of her defensive persona as a fierce, murdering animal. Her wounds are truly healed in every sense and as a complete person she can now move forward. She embodies the role of Dubh Ruis' wife, becomes a mother and integrates back into society and the community she abandoned after her father's death. Much later, when her beloved husband dies, she is able to navigate a 'healthy' grief process. Preparing his body, leading the ceremony for the community and freely expressing her grief and loss. Thus, she models an image of one experiencing grief and moving through it without being destroyed by it. Mis honours all she has learned with her husband during those formative months in the forest when they first met.

This again is likely to be a stage later down the process of managing loss when a significant amount of time and healing has passed. I have found seven years after the loss of my son I can now talk about it without getting upset and can relate to patients and colleagues who have been through similar. I feel empowered to offer my support, to those who wish it, who have lost a child and share what helped me through the process. I do feel contented in my life and optimistic about the future and I have learnt so much about navigating loss, disappointment and unexpected life stressors.

Are there ways that your experience could help others? Talking to people, writing a book or blog, maybe creating art to express the process of navigating loss. Hearing about lived experience is like finding treasure when you think you are the only person going through something awful. It is wonderful to feel seen and understood. Could you offer this to someone suffering in loss?

I hope these ideas have helped to form your thoughts around loss, consider how you have responded to loss in your life and how you could support others going through this. The Romance of Mis and Dubh Ruis is an exquisite and multilayered Celtic myth exploring this theme. I love the fierceness of Mis and the quiet confidence of Dubh Ruis. I also love how their healing and relationship developed slowly out of careful touch, music, play and eating and sleeping alongside each-other. No grand gestures or sweeping romantic quests to 'win' a marriage. These characters are now burnt in my brain, and I often consider when I need to be fierce and protective like Mis and when I need to be softer and more receptive like Dubh Ruis. The ending proves that soul wounds can indeed be healed and the divine relationship between these two characters offers us a powerful image of what that may look like.

The Wells of Blood
The Sumerian story of Inanna and Shukaletuda

Lindsay River

Many people interested in mythology are familiar with the story from ancient Mesopotamia of Inanna's descent to the Netherworld. In the Netherworld, you may recall, she is killed and hung on a hook, but revived by two magically made genderless beings who are able to slip through the gates and reach her with the water of life and the food of life.

Her death in the Netherworld is, of course, a terrible, indeed fatal, wounding but one which Inanna is able to overcome with the assistance of her faithful female vizier, Ninshubur, and the god of wisdom, Enki and the helpful beings he creates. Fewer people are aware of another myth of Inanna: the story of Inanna and the gardener Shukaletuda, where she is also deeply wounded. Perhaps surprisingly for this powerful goddess, the wound concerns sexual assault.

Here we must give a content warning, for Inanna's experience may resound for modern survivors. It may remind us of date rape drugging, of the exploitation of sick or disabled people, of many kinds of exploitation of varied bodies.

Yes, Inanna, the very goddess who inspires love and sexual desire in human beings and animals, who embodies Desire, in spite of the tremendous power that the Sumerians believed she possessed, is herself assaulted by a weak and criminal man. How then could this be? We must hear her story.

I intend to tell the story and to analyse it in two ways: the first to create a context for the reader who is not familiar with Sumerian culture. The other way is to begin to uncover what readings there may be for the modern reader. These will be ones that may not have been intended by the author of the text or the culture they drew the story from, but which the reader can discover in themself, co-authoring meaning with people from so long ago.

I will summarise the myth from a translation of the text that can be found on the Electronic Corpus of Sumerian Literature, which is provided online by the Faculty of Oriental Studies at Oxford University. I encourage you to read the original, for my story has changed it, has knitted together details to create flow and better understanding for the modern reader. The original story is repetitive and has some parts missing, but the main gist, with some rearrangement of order and interpretative readings of my own, is as follows below. Mine is a storyteller's retelling, not a translation, you must read the original (see note 1) to know what was actually in the text. As well as summarising I have added some sentences that seem to me explanatory for the modern reader.

The story seems likely to be an explanation of astronomical phenomena that were not only studied by the sky watching priests in Mesopotamia, but would have been apparent to many ordinary people. The planet Venus was believed to actually be the goddess Inanna. People could point to the planet, appearing as a very bright star, and feel that their goddess was watching over them. After telling the story and discussing it we will examine the astronomy that appears to underlie it.

The story tellers of Sumer told of what happened during one of Inanna's absences from the heavens, the story of Inanna and Shukaletuda, the shameful gardener.

Holy Inanna was a source of wonder, she had all the great divine powers (these were called the Me in Sumer) and she occupied the throne-dais in the famous E-anna temple in the city of Uruk. At some distance from Uruk was the city of Eridu, the city of the god Enki. His shrine at Eridu was a gateway to the abzu. (This was a mythic primeval freshwater sea under the earth from which lakes, rivers, and aquifers were thought to draw their waters). Eridu's shrine was famed and it was there in the backroom behind the shrine that Enki taught a raven, that highly intelligent corvid, how to grow plants and even trees. Yes, it was a raven, as the story tellers emphasized, and the Raven, though not human, was proficient and intelligent. The Raven followed Enki's instructions precisely, planting a mixture from the temple in a deep trench. From the Raven's conscientious work, a strange new plant grew up. It was a tall date palm which had multiple blessed uses for human beings – not only delicious dates and the heart of palm for food but fibers for weaving and for cleaning. Instructed by Enki, the Raven was also able to operate the shaduf, an irrigation device invented in Sumer that used counter weights to transfer water easily from a well to irrigation channels. The Raven, in spite of not being a human being, listened and learned well from the wise god Enki, so helping the fertility of the land and the wellbeing of the animals and people.

Inanna, who as the planet Venus could fly through the heavens, disappeared from her familiar path. She left her shrine in the E-anna and all her other shrines, her statues there were empty, no longer inhabited by the living goddess. She went up into the mountains. Her purpose there was to fulfill her role as a mighty judge, as the detector of falsehood and criminality, as protector of the just from the harm done by the unjust. When she reached the foot of the mountains she stood in power amongst the wild bulls that grazed there. None would harm her, they were her beasts. She climbed the mountains and stood amongst the stags that roamed the mountain tops. None would harm her, they too were her beasts.

Where the garden plots were being developed on the mountain there was a young man called Shukaletuda, the son of Igisigsig. His job was to water the garden plots and to install a well among the plants to improve its watering. But Shukaletuda did not have the efficiency, the wisdom of the Raven. He did not install and operate a shaduf. He did not even water the plants. There were no plants to water for he had pulled them out by their very roots, destroyed them completely. He was not a gardener, he was an anti-gardener. A storm wind blew on him then, blowing the unwatered dust of the mountains into his eyes. He looked to the lowlands and the dust gave him vision, he saw the exalted gods of the land where the sun rises. He looked to the highlands and saw the exalted gods of the land where the sun sets. He saw a solitary ghost. And then with his new vision he was able to recognise a deity who was completely alone, a being who possessed the divine powers. She was by a luxuriant and shady tree. It was in a plot near him that the tree grew. It was a Euphrates poplar, a blessed tree in that landscape where the sun could beat down mercilessly. It gave broad shade: effective in the morning when the sun shone from the east, it provided good cover in the heat of midday and its shade was not diminished in the evening when the sun sent its lower rays from the west.

Inanna was profoundly tired. She had crossed the heavens, she had circled the earth of Mesopotamia, she had visited other countries (Elam and Subir), she had gone around 'the intertwined horizon' as the story tellers said. She had climbed mountains. She was deeply, deeply exhausted and she lay down in the broad shade of the poplar, right by its roots.

Shukaletuda was watching her from his barren plot. He knew she was a deity. When he approached her, she was in a deep sleep. He saw the loincloth she wore, fabric that symbolised and embodied the seven divine powers she possessed, the Holy Me. These divine powers were intimately close to her, they covered her vulva, her vagina. Now Shukaletuda was not harmless like the bulls and the stags of the mountain. He undid the loincloth of the Me, exposing her genitals (we can assume this was as she slept). Then he got her to lie back down under the tree. In the depth of her exhaustion she did not know that he kissed her, that he forced intercourse upon her. Then Shukaletuda went back to his plot, but knowing his guilt, he did not stay there. He went home to his father.

The sun rose, and Inanna woke. She knew something was wrong but she did not know what it was. She inspected her body closely. There was evidence of an assault. She struggled to comprehend what had happened. She was shocked, she was troubled, she was grieved, she was enraged. She was considering what or who would now have to be punished, destroyed because of what had happened to her. What should be done?

Her pain overwhelmed her. All the wells, with their shadoufs bringing water to the thirsty land, bringing water to the thirsty people, no longer brought water, they were filled with blood. It was blood that irrigated the orchards where the sacred apple trees grew. It was blood that women drew from the well for the family. It was blood that the people of Sumer drank. It was a terrible plague and nobody knew when it would end. Inanna did not herself know how to end it. She knew now what had happened and she said: "I will search everywhere for the man who had intercourse with me". But nowhere in all the lands could she find the man. She who inspected the land to find the wrongdoer, she who protected those who were harmed, alas she now could not find the perpetrator of her own rape.

Shukaletuda was at home with his father. He told the whole story, his failure as a gardener, the storm-wind with its dust and the magical visionary properties it afforded, the poplar with its broad shade and the goddess beneath the tree, Inanna's deep sleeping, his removal of the loincloth of the Me, the unspeakable assault. Then Inanna's waking and the manifestation of bleeding wells all over the land.

Did his father counsel Shukaletuda to go to a High Priestess of Inanna and confess his crime? He did not. He did not think how the people could be saved from drinking blood or how the Holy Goddess Inanna could be comforted or healed. Instead, he reacted immediately to protect and hide the wrongdoer, his son. He told him to hide amongst the city dwellers 'your brothers'. He insisted that Shukaletuda should not be visible to Inanna by being anywhere among the mountains or the plots where he had been gardening. Inanna could not find him.

She considered her situation again. She was troubled, she was in pain, now she was hugely enraged. She mounted on a great cloud and it became her steed. The south wind and a fearsome storm flood went before her. Behind her came a great dust storm and a powerful retainer from her temple: the pilipili, one of her cultic personnel. She was also followed by her advisers and seven times seven of her personnel stood beside in her in the high desert. She swore that she would search everywhere for the man who had intercourse with her without her consent. But nowhere could she find him. Shukaletuda's father, consulted by the anxious perpetrator, insisted again he hide among the city dwellers 'your brothers'. So again he hid.

Inanna considered a third time what should be done. This time she blocked the highways of the land. The perpetrator would not be able to dodge from place to place. Yet nowhere still could Inanna find her attacker.

Shukaletuda's father insisted again he remain among the city dwellers, hidden, 'among your brothers'.

The next daybreak Inanna inspected herself closely again. She felt strongly she must have justice, she should surely be compensated for what happened to her. Inanna set off then to the abzu in Eridu, the shrine that led to the primeval fresh waters beneath the earth. This was where Enki, her spiritual father was to be found.

Powerful goddess that she was, she prostrated herself on the ground before him and stretched out her hands to him: "Father Enki, I should be compensated! Someone should pay for what happened to me! I shall only re-enter my shrine in the E-anna once I have that man in my power.

Enki knew how bad her prolonged absence would be for the people of Uruk. He was moved by her suffering. "So be it!" He pronounced.

Inanna now was given a new divine ability. She stretched herself across the sky forming a great arc, like a rainbow. She let the south wind pass across her, she let the north wind pass across her. Shukaletuda now was alone and terrified and he tried to make himself as small as possible so that Inanna overhead could not see him. But from the great rainbow-like arc that she had become there was no hiding. She saw him, she knew exactly who he was and what he had done. She swore at him, calling him names of disgust.

Shukaletuda tried to tell his story again as some kind of explanation just as he had done to his father. He recounted his experience of the garden and the storm wind, and he concluded by saying that Inanna, exhausted, was lying down to rest under the shady poplar. He left out the way he had controlled the sleeping goddess, he left out the fact he had certainly known what he was doing, he left out that he removed the loincloth with the Holy Me from her body, he concluded by saying that he had intercourse with her there under the poplar before going back to his plot.

Inanna drew herself up into her role as the great judge. She delivered her judgment. She determined his destiny, and it was his death. She rested.

Commentary

This then is the bones of the story, with some interpretive explanation of my own. It ends with a section that appears to me to be an interpolation from the storyteller or singer that is telling the tale as entertainment. I believe it may be included to create a happier ending, to make the song and story more attractive for performers and audiences For the last words of the goddess that are comprehensible in the text are said to be:

'So! You shall die! What is that to me? Your name, however, shall not be forgotten. Your name shall exist in songs and make the songs sweet."

This emphasis on the sweetness to the hearer, and it is the male hearers that are then mentioned, seems also to be a kind of promotion of the art of the storyteller. While many Sumerian listeners might consider the immortality accorded to Shukaletuda made his death worthwhile (in a culture that valued immortality of one's name very highly), can we believe that every female listener found the song as sweet? Or any person who had been similarly abused, whatever their gender? It is impossible to tell: any variations in the reception of traditional stories have to remain unknown to us. There must have been variations according to gender and status, for women, male and female slaves and bonded servants, eunuchs and those defeated in war were particularly vulnerable to being raped.

For the many modern readers however, the supposed sweetness of the story strikes very strangely, it might even offend. However, there is for many readers a kind of enjoyment, a satisfaction that Inanna was apparently released from her distress by finding and punishing her rapist, in seeing that justice was done. We too have films and books that recount an assault and the search of the survivor for justice, they are clearly attractive to us as watchers and readers who also yearn for the punishment of the wrongdoer. Yet this is a complicated enjoyment which the simple words of the Sumerian text do not seem to reflect to the modern reader. For me as a modern reader, as a survivor, I question my own attraction to this story of Inanna, to all stories of assault and revenge. I question it with kindness towards myself, with empathy, with some understanding. And that is I think another kind of sweetness, one that is not towards the perpetrator whose name lives on, but to the survivor who feels with Inanna, and to the goddess herself.

There are vast cultural and historical differences in our understanding of this tale and how it may have been understood by the Sumerians. Yet in spite of this there are key points of the story which may speak to the modern reader. We need to balance awareness of our 'not-knowing' (because we are not a Sumerian audience) with our knowing based on our own experience and that of people in our society. It is important to realise that this is not only the story of a woman's experience we can identify with, it is a mythic story of the gods in a profoundly different society from ours. Both are true. It seems likely from various pointers that we are being shown that Shukaletuda has violated divine ordinances, that the rape is both actual and symbolic. To start with Inanna is not only 'a woman' (as the text often refers to her) she is a goddess, replete with the divine powers, and the text emphasises that. The tree she lays down beneath is a sacred tree, a tree that provides shade at all times of day, a tree of immense value to the Sumerian people.

She wears a loincloth that both symbolized and embodied the Holy Me, the ordinances of the divine order given to the Sumerians by the gods. Shukaletuda removes this without her knowledge or consent, while she is sleeping the sleep of divine exhaustion. (I believe the exhaustion she is experiencing is implied to be like the unconsciousness brought about by drink or drugs). She had circled the heavens and the earth, and visited cities where her most famous shrines were based at the time of the storytelling. These were considered to be actions of hers which help to keep the universe in balance, for the planet Venus, which she inhabits/is, follows a predictable course and contributes to divine harmony. While this was, of course, a sexual assault, to the Sumerians it would also be blasphemous because of the importance of the Holy Me, because of the assault on a goddess with the highest divine powers, wearing the symbol of the cosmic ordinances, under a sacred and valuable tree.

At the same time this is a story that necessarily resonates with many women and people of other genders who have been abused. We need not only regard his action as particularly criminal in the eyes of the Sumerians because Inanna is a goddess. We can read this as emphasising by analogy the 'blasphemy' of non-consensual sex, the rape of an unconscious person.

Inanna's experience recounted here, millennia ago, brings to mind vividly the story told in *I May Destroy You* by Michaela Coel, the award-winning Ghanaian-British actress, filmmaker, singer, and composer. This is a TV series based on the main character, Arabella's, gradual discovery that she has been given a date-rape drug by a supposed friend and raped in the toilet of a club. Like Coel's character, Inanna is not immediately sure what has happened. Something is wrong, her body is telling her something has happened, something terrible in the most intimate area. She has to keep checking to be sure of this. Perhaps like Arabella, she has some vague dream memory that becomes more clear as time passes. In the same way she comes to the realization that she has been violated. But who is the man? Inanna does not know but with her divine powers she will be able to recognise him if she can find him. However, a patriarchal and fraternal collusion has set in. Shukaletuda realises his guilt and his predicament: having not only committed rape but of a goddess who was equipped with the symbols of high divine office. His father has no regard for the justice and truth that Inanna presides over when she sits in judgment on her shining throne. He tells his son to go the city and hide amongst men who would collude with him, 'his brothers'. This, of course, is a tactic often used by sexual predators today: they leave the countryside where they can more easily be identified by reputation or local social networks, and go to a distant city where they can hide their identity and their past.

Inanna is herself a most elevated divine judge. A hymn to Inanna from around 1900 BCE was written for Iddin-Dagon, a king of Isin, who, as a mortal representative of Dumuzi, was regarded as the spouse of Inanna in a sacred marriage. The hymn describes Inanna's role as a judge when she is seen as a morning star, the Lady of the Morning. People requiring judgements are described as assembling before dawn when the planet Venus is in the sky.

> When all the lands and people of Sumer assemble,
> Those sleeping on the roofs and those sleeping by the
> walls,
> When they sing your praises, bringing their concerns to
> you,
> You study their words.
>
> You render a cruel judgement against the evildoer,
> You destroy the wicked.
> You look with kindly eyes on the straightforward;
> You give that one your blessing.

A judge herself, she now needs to bring her own attacker to justice. Ironically, divine judge though she is, she cannot locate him. She is consumed by pain, grief and rage. So it is that a plague falls upon the people of Sumer: all the wells no longer give water, but blood. People are forced to drink it, to use it for watering their crops and their livestock. Blood is pulled up and tipped upon the land by the shadouf. Here we see a direct reference to Shukaletuda, though Inanna does not know his name. He was the failed gardener who was meant to install a well to improve the watering of his plot. I do not see Inanna's filling the wells with blood as a simple act of vengeance on the people of Sumer, though, make no mistake, Inanna is capable of huge anger: she destroys a mountain that does not bow to her. Rather I read it as an inevitable consequence of Inanna's pain, of her damaged body, of the desecration of the wellspring that is her genitals (and next to which in one poem after Dumuzi has consensual sex with her, plants spring up at their sides). We could perhaps compare the plague of the bloody wells with the barren earth that follows when, in much later Greek myth, Demeter is grieving the rape and loss of her beloved Persephone. While Demeter is an earth goddess, many devotees of Inanna are not happy with the simplistic description of Inanna as a 'fertility goddess'. Indeed, this appellation has been used to by some Assyriologists and commentators of myth in the past to avoid mentioning her abundant and explicit sexuality, and the way she manifests this in acts of lovemaking. They have focussed on the implied economic and social products of that sexuality: fertility of the land, fertility of the people and their livestock. Inanna is not a Mother Goddess (her 'sons' Shara and Lulal are probably lesser gods of different cities where Inanna is worshipped), she is not a grain goddess as such, she is not 'Mother Earth'. She is however, especially in her earlier manifestations when she was associated with the date store, the orchard, the garden and the sheepfold, intimately connected with the land. When the god Dumuzi is courting Inanna, he brings her into his garden. Both of them refer to fields and the word vulva also means furrow. Inanna cries out in the poem *The Courtship of Inanna and Dumuzi*

> My untilled land lies fallow.
> As for me, Inanna,
> Who will plow my vulva?
> Who will plow my high field?
> Who will plow my wet ground?
> As for me, the young woman,
> Who will plow my vulva?

Who will station the ox there?
Who will plow my vulva?

Dumuzi, her 'honey man' who 'sweetens her always' answers
that he will plow her vulva.

Inanna answers enthusiastically:

Then plow my vulva, man of my heart!
Plow my vulva!

At the king's lap stood the rising cedar.
Plants grew high by their side.
Grains grew high by their side.
Gardens flourished luxuriantly.

The gardens flourished, unlike Shukaletuda's plots. Inanna
describes her courtship with her 'brother'. ('Brother' in this
context means that Dumuzi is an equal with Inanna, not that
he is to be seen as her biological brother). Dumuzi's sexual
excitement is compared to the poplar tree, no doubt the very
same Euphrates poplar that Inanna lies under in the Shukaletuda
myth. Inanna speaks:

He brought me into his garden
My brother, Dumuzi, brought me into his garden
I strolled with him among the standing trees,
I stood with him among the fallen trees
By an apple tree I knelt as is proper.
Before my brother coming in song,
Who rose to me out of the poplar leaves.

Consensual sex, initiated by the Goddess' own request, brings
fertility. Dumuzi sang:

O Lady, your breast is your field.
Inanna, your breast is your field.
Your broad field pours out plants
Your broad field pours out grain.
Water flows from on high for your servant.
Bread flows from on high for your servant.
Pour it out for me, Inanna.
I will drink all you offer.

The contrast between the barren and the flourishing gardens, between Dumuzi and Shukaletuda, could not be greater. Non-consensual sex perpetrated on an unconscious and exhausted goddess by a failed gardener, leads only to wells of blood that could not refresh the people. The assault on her sleeping body is vividly reflected in the land. The land cries out with her pain. Her genitals are bruised (which is I believe how we are to read the repeated phrase in the original text 'because of her genitals'). The bloody wells are a vivid statement of Inanna's subjective experience.

Inanna becomes more certain of what has happened to her. No longer confused by sleep or immobilised by the shock of discovering that an assault occurred while she was unconscious, she prepares for battle. She is the Lady of Battle and she harnesses the elements that are at her command. For Inanna had power over storms. It was a fit symbol of her rage that she mounted on a cloud and was preceded by the South wind and a fearsome storm flood. (Iraq can be hit by monsoon type rains that cause great floods). Behind Inanna came another kind of storm, a dust storm. These storms are created when strong winds lift areas of sand and dry earth, they have tremendous consequences in terms of human health, affecting breathing and causing long term damage. The South wind mentioned before is probably a reference to what is called in modern Arabic the sharqī which blows from the south and southeast during early summer and early winter and brings terrible dust storms that can rise to an enormous height in the atmosphere. With the dust storm travelled the pilipili – a figure who is one of the cultic personnel in Inanna's entourage and was the title of some of those who worked in her temples. The pilipili is described in one text as the 'reed marsh dweller', which can be read as one who is betwixt and between, neither on water nor on land, and who is one who Inanna had changed from woman into man. In this mythic context we can expect this pilipili to be an original, mythic, most powerful pilipili after whom the human workers in her temples are named. With her forty-nine assistants beside in her in the high desert, and with the enraged elements, Inanna's forces are awesome indeed.

Yet still she cannot find the perpetrator. He is still hiding. So, a third time Inanna's pain, grief, rage and desire for justice are expressed. She blocks the highways. These roads between cities and villages would likely be the only ones that could be taken, the only ones where water could be found en route, where food could be obtained by travellers. If they could not be used, no trade could take place and the economies of cities were in danger of collapse. No food, no resources could be transported from place to place. The cities were not self-sufficient, they needed food to be brought from the countryside to feed their large populations. People would become hungry. It was a disaster for humankind in Mesopotamia. Once again Shukaletuda appeals to his father, who repeats his advice.

Inanna goes now to Enki, the wise god, and she is successful at last. Enki helps her, gives her the power to form a rainbow-like arch across the whole landscape, and she is able to find Shukaletuda. Inanna, who had the power to rouse desire, to make desire die down, who was the very essence of sexuality to the people of Mesopotamia, who ruled all kinds of sex and desire (as her temple rituals imply to those who study them) did not allow sex without consent. Shukaletuda could not attempt to bring any defence that she was so attractive, so magically able to rouse desire, that he was unable to resist her beauty though she was asleep and exhausted. In the light of her shining presence, he could not and Inanna would have regarded it with no mercy.

I take this myth far more seriously than some of its commentators. Jeffrey Cooley, whose article I discuss below, says that one commentator saw it as 'darkly comic' as the terrified Shukaletuda hides from the enraged Inanna We could compare this with the dark comedy in Coel's, *I May Destroy You*. But this myth has not been accorded very much interest. It should be far better known.

Let us now look at the theory that this myth relates to the movements of the planet Venus in the sky. I believe this to be correct. It is already known that the Descent of Inanna to the Netherworld was related to the planet Venus's 'synodic period'. This is the cycle during which the planet appears as Morning Star, then disappears for some months (her superior conjunction with the Sun, whose light makes her invisible to observers), then reappears as an Evening Star, appears to move backwards (retrograde) and then disappears again into the horizon at inferior conjunction for days or weeks depending on the time of year, before re-emerging as Morning Star again. The cycle does not recur annually but rather every 584 days (just over nineteen months/one year and seven months). The movements of the planet Venus, often a very bright object in a clear sky, would have been familiar to most people in ancient Mesopotamia, and watched by many., They would know well that Venus appeared either as a morning star or an evening star, in alternation, with periods of disappearance in between. As a morning star in the east before dawn she called people to wake and prepare for the working day, when she appeared as an evening star in the west after sunset, she heralded a time of rest and enjoyment and the delights of love.

Jeffrey Cooley, in an article on the myth of Inanna and Shukaletuda, expands on a previous suggestion to propose a conjectural link between this cycle and the myth. It is possible indeed that over the great length of time that Inanna/Ishtar was worshiped (over three millennia at least) and the planet Venus watched (over two millennia at least) in the region, a variety of myths were developed to explain the planet's movements which were quite different from those of Mars, Jupiter and Saturn. The disappearance of protective Inanna/Venus was of great significance to the Sumerians and the Akkadians who followed them.

Following Jeffrey Cooley, when Inanna comes to rest under the Euphrates poplar, she (as the planet Venus) has been moving through the Western sky every evening after sunset for about eight months. Now as the planet disappears from view on the horizon the goddess needs rest but instead, she has the fateful unconscious encounter with the abusive Shukaletuda. When she becomes visible again, she searches for her attacker. We can associate her varied efforts to find him with the approximately eight months the planet appears in the eastern morning sky before dawn. We know this morning manifestation was linked by the Sumerians with her role as a dispenser of divine justice. When she cannot find him after all best efforts, she goes to visit the god Enki in his shrine in the city of Eridu, the gateway to the abzu or imagined waters under the earth. Cooley is unsure whether this could relate to the planet Venus's disappearance for some months at superior conjunction with the sun, as her trip to the abzu appears a fairly quick one in the tale. However, the passing of time in the myth is not very clear – the eight months that would have passed as she searches is also not clear. I believe that it does relate to this superior conjunction disappearance because in other work I have done, I have found a connection between Inanna's visit to Enki and the abzu with Venus's behaviour at superior conjunction.

What then does the arching of Inanna across the land 'like a rainbow' correspond to? Jeffrey Cooley theorises that this relates to the fact that the movements of Venus are always only on the Western or Eastern horizon, the planet never makes an arc across the whole sky. Therefore, he reasons, she cannot see Shukaletuda, who is lurking in the city in the middle of the landscape. Yet, empowered by Enki, she is miraculously able to make this arc across the sky, a rainbow-like span from East to West that can be crossed by the winds from both South and from North. This part of the myth does not relate to an actual astronomical event, for Venus can in fact never do this. It is a fantastic mythic outcome allowed by Enki. However it may relate to a new development in the way Inanna/Ishtar was understood. The so-called "Great God-List" includes the deification of the rainbow as the Goddess Manzât, and she is part of the retinue of deities associated with Ishtar. A colleague has drawn my attention to this and suggests that the Rainbow Goddess could possibly be seen as a manifestation of Ishtar rather than an independent deity. He points out that Shukaletuda was assumed to be safe in the city because the Mesopotamians regarded all their cities as 'the centre of the world' and hence safe from Ishtar who appeared on the horizons, not overhead. This part of the story could be explaining by implication that Enki accorded to Inanna/Ishtar the ability to manifest as Manzât, to become her, and arch overhead, thus being able to see the perpetrator below.

What does any of this theoretical astronomical connection matter to us as readers of her myth in the light of the wounding, the assaults on and the power to survive of goddesses and other mythological figures? I believe it is very significant. It indicates to me that at some time, somewhere in Sumer or in the civilisations that followed it, the myth of the assault on Inanna by Shukaletuda was considered to be of importance, it was considered to be related to the goddess' absence when Venus was not in the sky. It was therefore to be compared to her more famous descent into the Netherworld, her survival of death there, assisted by the god Enki, and her return in triumph. There is a similar theme of survival of great trauma.

The whole process from the assault to the finding of Shukaletuda would have taken about a year, the larger portion of the planet's 19-month cycle. Even Inanna, Queen of Heaven and of Earth, with all her superpowers, is affected this long. While this could be a depressing thought, I see it as acknowledging survivors, recognising our struggle. I see the wells of blood as manifestations of the goddess' pain, I see Inanna on her storm cloud, followed by her gender-changed acolyte the pili-pili and accompanied by dust storms and other manifestations, as a recognition of the validity of the survivor's rage.

It is significant that these events take place in a garden or in adjacent garden plots. In this case an assault on the Queen of Heaven occurs in garden plots where the gardener himself has pulled up plants, and failed to install watering. It is not the only story from this region of a garden in which terrible events occur. In the story of Enki and Ninhursag we see an earlier version of the god Enki who is not wise, who seduces his own young female descendants and eats up all the fruit that the Mother Goddess, Ninhursag, has created. It has been suggested that themes from this creation myth may have contributed to the Garden of Eden story. The story of Inanna and Shukaletuda can be seen as another version of the garden. It is possible that even more variant myths of gardens exist, but have not yet been discovered in written form (thousands of cuneiform tablets are waiting to be translated, or may never yet have been dug up).

I see the final outcome of Inanna and Shukaletuda as recognition that even if it seems that a miracle will be required in the face of patriarchal collusions, the survivor of abuse must be centred in the story, and must find justice (one appropriate to their time and place). It is a myth that may perhaps have spoken to many women, and people of all genders, over millennia. It can speak to us today.

Sulis – Healing Your Own Curses

Rachel Patterson

Sulis is an ancient English goddess and one of the few we have at least some evidence of thanks in the most part to the Romans. From archaeological evidence we know that she was worshiped at the natural hot springs in Bath, Somerset, England going back at least to the Mesolithic period. Unfortunately, there do not seem to be any myths or legends passed down about her, so we have had to work from history found at the Romans Baths and springs alongside a few mentions of her in ancient Roman documents.

The spring is the only natural hot spring in the British Isles and is believed to be over 12000 years old, basically from the end of the last ice age. The water filters down through limestone in the Mendip hills, through the clay and mudstone of the hills and valleys and rises up under the city of Bath. The waters are not just thermal, they are packed with at least 38 minerals, all of which contributes to the belief the waters were healing.

Worship of the goddess has been found in the form of stone tools in the mud of the springs dating back to the Mesolithic period. As humans we have a habit of throwing things into water of all kinds, it is believed these stone tool heads were given as offerings. Other items show the springs were visited regularly from that point onwards until about 5000 to 6000 years ago when the area around it was just used as farmland. It is unclear as to why people stopped visiting at that point, perhaps only spiritual leaders were then allowed near the springs.

Once the Romans arrived, loving their bathing as they did, they built a spa to incorporate the hot springs. Realizing the local spring water goddess, Sulis was well respected and revered, they adopted her. The Romans even named the town Aquae Sulis, or 'waters of Sulis'.

A temple was built inside the bath structure to honor and worship the goddess Sulis and it was a pretty impressive building. A pediment towered above the steps supported on four high columns. Adorning the pediment is a centre piece that has been named 'the gorgon' as it was initially thought to be an image of a gorgon head. No one really knows who or what it is, but I like to think of it as an image of the solar god Belenus, watching guard over the temple of Sulis. More imagery on the pediment includes a wreath of oak leaves, an eight-pointed star, Victories (winged messengers from the gods), Tritons (demi gods of the sea), helmets, an owl and a dolphin.

Inside her temple was a larger-than-life size bronze statue of Sulis, or Sulis Minerva as the Roman's renamed her. The statue would have looked down over an altar that was used for ceremonies and sacrifice. Offerings and petitions were thrown into the hot spring pool that was also within the temple boundaries.

It is believed that the temple housed a sacred flame to Sulis that was kept alight at all times.

Coins seem to have been the favourite offerings to the spring waters, nearly 13000 having been recovered so far. Personal items are also included such as bracelets and earrings along with gemstones. Plenty of pewter items are included such as bowls and small dishes, often with inscriptions dedicating the item to Sulis.

Most famous though are the curse tablets, 130 of them have been uncovered (so far). Each one comprising of a small piece of lead or pewter with the request written with a metal point and then the petition folded or rolled before being sent into the waters. Nearly all of these are requests for vengeance.

Whilst there is not much information on how Sulis was worshipped or what she was worshipped for, most modern folk see her as a healing goddess because of the spring waters. She is also seen as a solar goddess because of the heat of the water. I do agree that one of her facets is as a healing goddess, more importantly for me, I look to the large number of curses that were sent her way. No evidence has been found of any requests for healing (at least not yet) which further adds to my belief that she was more likely a goddess of justice and vengeance. But you can take your own view as you see fit.

My journey with Sulis began back in 2009 on a visit to Bath for a short break. It was during that trip that we visited the Roman Baths just as a lot of tourists do. It was a hauntingly magical experience, and she has been with me ever since. Each subsequent visit (and there have been a few) has reinforced my connection not only to Sulis but also to the god Belenus.

She is the goddess I call upon when I need strength but also if something needs some kick butt kind of action to get things going or move things along quickly. She moves fast, she takes no prisoners, she suffers no fools and gets the job done.

Originally, before the Romans she would probably have been the 'spirit of the waters' with no real form. But when she comes to me now, she seems to have fully embraced the Roman way of life, look and appearance. I get the feeling, actually I don't just get the feeling, I know, that she likes to dress in the regalia and have attention paid to her. She is the only goddess that I have ever felt the need to address formally as 'm'lady'. And boy does she love the finer things in life! You, of course, may feel otherwise in your encounters with her. But as we have no records to go on, you need to trust your own intuition and experiences with her.

My altars to Sulis are always dressed in bright yellows and reds to reflect the solar nature but with flashes of blue and green to correspond with the natural spring waters. I haven't found any specific statues or ornaments depicting Sulis so I go with artwork instead, I have two that I love, one by Suzi Edwards

Goose (the Ink Witch) and another by Naomi of Nomeart. I also have several items that I purchased in the Roman Baths gift shop; a plaque depicting the 'gorgon head', some Roman tiles showing the same image, a boar and the head of the bronze Sulis Minerva statue and, of course, a bottle of spring water. Images of the sun are also useful to have, and you can get all sorts of offering dishes and candle holders with solar imagery. Representations of water are good whether that is in the form of a dish of water or something like shells or river pebbles.

Images of the Roman Baths work well too, particularly as a 'backdrop'.

Coins are good to have as offerings, modern coins are perfectly acceptable, but I also have some replica Roman coins.

Mosaic designs are lovely to have on your altar to Sulis, the Romans in particular loved their mosaic floors.

Images or representations of dolphins or owls to reflect the imagery in the pediment artwork although I personally feel owls have a stronger connection to Minerva than Sulis.

As it appears her temple had a sacred flame, then candles obviously are perfect to have on your altar to Sulis.

I like to start my altar by blessing and consecrating it with water, of course. Charge a bowl of water under the mid-day sun to add the solar element then clean your altar with it.

Dress your altar with an altar cloth then add the items you feel drawn to put there, trust your intuition it will never let you down.

When making a petition to Sulis I like to replicate the idea of a pewter curse tablet by writing on slips of aluminium foil.

Offerings should always be made when you have asked her for help, guidance or assistance, it is only fair to give something in return for her services. I use coins, herbs, flowers, shells and sometimes beads. Wine and grapes also work well.

One of the best ways to connect with Sulis is to take a bath, it really is a simple way to make that connection.

As with any deity you will need to build a relationship, this will take time and effort. Do your research, read up about the Roman Baths and find your connection to her. Look at images online that depict her temple and the offerings made to her. If you get the chance, I highly recommend visiting the city of Bath and the Roman Baths.

Meditate with the purpose of meeting her and build a relationship and dialogue with her. Create an altar to honor her, light candles to her and give offerings.

And now to the curses, obviously if you want to set curses then Sulis is the perfect goddess to do so with, but only you can make that decision. What I do believe she is excellent to work with for is releasing us from the curses we place upon ourselves.

We restrict ourselves; we constantly remind ourselves that we are no good, or not worthy or unable to do particular things or that we cannot do something. These are curses we place on ourselves. Sulis can help us to change the way we think and treat ourselves.

Water has a reflective surface particularly in the stillness of a bath, we can see true reflections of ourselves and how we treat our own self in that surface.

Sulis can hold up that 'water mirror' and show us just how badly we have been mistreated, by our own doing.

Sulis Ritual for Self-Reflection

It is really important when you are casting a circle and calling the quarters to visualise, otherwise you are just saying words. See the circle forming around you and see and feel the elements joining you in the sacred space.

You will need:

A candle for Sulis and a lighter

Four candles, one for each direction
A shallow bowl
Water
A silver coin

Take a calm, peaceful bath to begin with. Then dress in something comfortable.

Cast a circle by walking clockwise around, if you have flower petals you can sprinkle them around to form your sacred space.

As you cast the circle, say:

Sulis, goddess of power and might
Protect this circle around us and shine your light.

Repeat the chant three times.

Welcome in the elements and light a candle at each direction.

Begin in the North:

Element of earth I welcome you and ask that you bring stability.
I welcome you.

Facing east:

Element of air I welcome you and ask that you bring intuition.
I welcome you.

Facing south:

Element of fire, I welcome you and ask that you bring passion.
I welcome you.

Facing west:

> *Element of water, I welcome you and ask that you bring balance*
> *of emotions.*
> *I welcome you.*

Turning to the center, light a candle to honor Sulis and say:

> *Lady of the springs, Sulis, goddess of the solar waters, I call*
> *upon you and ask that you lend your energy to the ritual. In*
> *the hope that you will shine your light and give me insight.*

Now fill your bowl with water and drop a silver coin into the waters.

Sit the bowl in front of the Sulis candle and sit quietly.

Position yourself so that you can see your own reflection in the surface of the water.

Ask Sulis to give you guidance and insight, what do you do to curse yourself and how can you remedy it.

Listen to any messages you hear or images you see.

When you are ready face the center and thank Sulis and ask her to continue to guide you going forward.

Now release the quarters in reverse order.

Facing west:

> *Element of water I thank you for lending your energy to this*
> *ritual.*
> *I thank you for your presence.*

Facing south:

> *Element of fire I thank you for lending your energy to this*
> *ritual.*

I thank you for your presence.

Facing east:

> *Element of air I thank you for lending your energy to this ritual.*
> *I thank you for your presence.*

Facing north:

> *Element of earth I thank you for lending your energy to this ritual.*
> *I thank you for your presence.*

Walking anti clockwise around the circle, say:

> *With my thanks to the solar goddess Sulis, this circle is now uncast.*

Pour the water onto the earth as thanks. Keep the silver coin with you as a reminder to think about your reflection and how you treat yourself.

Sulis will guide and support you as you learn to be kinder to yourself. Remove those curses that you have already placed upon yourself but she will also show you how to learn to stop them before they happen.

Listen to her, learn from her and walk beside her.

The Embrace of Ereshkigal

Frances Billinghurst

When it comes to working with Deity, one thing that I have come to realise over the years is that not everything is what it may seem. And when you add the aspect of healing into the mix, well, that can take things to a completely different dimension. This was definitely my experience with respect to the Goddess whom I have chosen to write about for this anthology – that being the formidable ruler of the Sumerian Underworld, Ereshkigal, the "Great Lady under the Earth", who is more commonly associated with the dead as opposed to assisting the living. Before I share my healing story, I feel there is a need to first provide some background about Ereshkigal.

Hailing from the lands the ancient Greeks referred to as Mesopotamia (meaning "the land between two rivers", between the Tigris and Euphrates and what is modern day Iraq), Ereshkigal is better known through the ancient poem, "The Descent of the Goddess". Considered to be one of the oldest recorded poems, composed sometime between 3,500 BCE and 1,900 BCE, it recounts what happens to Inanna when she decides to enter Ereshkigal's realm, that of the Great Below, in order to witness funerary rites relating to the Bull of Heaven known as Gugalanna.

According to the various interpretations of the cuneiform fragments of this ancient poem, such as that found within *Inanna: Queen of Heaven and Earth*, when Ereshkigal is made aware of Inanna's arrival, she demands all seven gates to her realm to be locked so that the Queen of Heaven, who had decided to dress herself with all her symbols of status, is only allowed admittance after surrendering an item that connects her to the Upper World. This means that each time

Inanna steps through a gate, she is forced to relinquish a status symbol, starting with the Crown of Heaven that connects her to the cosmos, and ending with either her robe or loin cloth (undergarments). When these instructions are relayed, the Queen of Heaven exclaims over and over again at each gate that she comes to: "What is this?", only to be told: "Be quiet, Inanna. The ways of the Underworld are perfect. They may not be questioned." Eventually Inanna crosses the threshold of the seventh and final gate, and enters the chamber "naked and bent low" alluding to the possibility that this gate is perhaps smaller than the others. Here Ereshkigal is waiting for her, along with the Anunnaki, the divine judges of the Underworld, who cast judgment upon Inanna. Ereshkigal then directs the "words of wraith" and fastens her death stare upon the Queen of Heaven, killing her. Inanna's corpse is placed on a hook for three days and three nights before her trusted handmaiden, Ninshubur, seeks the assistance from the other Gods. Inanna is eventually rescued by the kurgarra and the galatur, two sexless creatures fashioned by her father, Enki, from dirt under his fingernails. These creatures are able to restore Inanna back to life, enabling her to ascend back to the Upper World naturally somewhat transformed by her experience.

The modern interpretations of this myth often tend to favor the beautiful and youthful Inanna over Ereshkigal, with the latter, although never actually described in historic sources, being described as somewhat hideous, or even skeletal, in appearance, and thus, whose treatment towards the Queen of Heaven has been alluded to be based on jealousy, anger and unjustified vengeance. Yet, as I mentioned earlier, things are not always as they seem.

When I started exploring Ereshkigal in preparation for my book about the Dark Goddess, my research saw me delve deeper into her own story, contained amongst the scattered fragments of cuneiform script that fell outside of "The

Descent of the Goddess" myth, as well as within the pages of rather dry academic writings. This resulted in a different and possible explanation as to her treatment of Inanna, through the connection of what appeared to be backstories, not to mention how Ereshkigal became connected with the Great Below in the first place.

The first myth is contained within the *Epic of Gilgamesh*, a collection of five poems dating back to possibly between 2,112 to around 2,000 BCE about a hero who may have even been an earlier Sumerian king who became deified. The earliest of these poems, *Gilgamesh, Enkidu, and the Netherworld*, tell of how the hero Gilgamesh, together with his friend Enkidu, come to the aid of the beautiful Inanna in order to drive out creatures who have taken up residence in her huluppu tree. These creatures include a serpent "who knows no charm", the Anzû-bird (thought to be a lion headed eagle often found within Mesopotamian art), and a demon referred to as Lilitu, the forerunner to the rather controversial goddess, Lilith.

A later poem in this collection mentions the hero spurning the Queen of Heaven's sexual advances by reminding her of the misery that her previous lovers had endured at her own hands. This sends Inanna into a "bitter rage" where she demands that her father, Anu, defend her honour by sending Gugalanna, the Bull of Heaven, to battle Gilgamesh. Initially, Anu refuses, reminding his daughter that she deserved to receive such comments due to her "abominable behaviour". Eventually, however, Inanna manages to manipulate her father in order for her wishes to be met. The desired outcome is not realised as, with the aid of his friend Enkidu, Gilgamesh is victorious over Gugalanna, and the Bull of Heaven is killed instead. This backstory sheds additional light on the funerary rites that Inanna seeks to witness in her own story. What is often left out of the discussion is the fact that Gugalanna, the Bull of Heaven, is actually the husband of Ereshkigal. As such, this provides a reason as to why the Queen of the Great Below reacts in the manner she did upon learning the unwanted arrival of Inanna to the gates of her realm. When it comes to how Ereshkigal became the ruler of the Great Below, things are less clear. In his interpretation of "Gilgamesh, Enkidu and the Netherworld" contained within Sumerian Mythology: A Study of Spiritual and Literary Achievement in the Third Millennium BCE, 3 Samuel Noah Kramer makes mention of an introductory passage to the "Epic of Gilgamesh" of Ereshkigal being abducted by the Kur (sometimes described as monster) and is taken into the Underworld where she becomes his queen.

When her brother, Enki, the God of Water, sets out in a boat to slay the Kur, his boat is pelted with rocks. Despite no victor of the battle being declared, Enki is implied as being victorious and descends into the Underworld. From the poem fragment, it appears that Enki never actually retrieves his sister. In fact, all he returns to the surface with are seeds for the huppulu tree that he subsequently plants along the banks of the Euphrates River. Is this the same tree that Inanna later finds inhabited with creatures? Further, while we do not know what happened to the Kur, Ereshkigal apparently remains in the Underworld, where she becomes its ruler.

This abduction of Ereshkigal appears to have a number of similarities to another abduction story – that of the Greek maiden, Kore, who was also seized by an Underworldly character, this case Hades, the Lord of the Underworld. In the Greek myth, Kore was transformed into Persephone, who was also described as a formidable Goddess, and becomes a co-ruler of the Underworld. A further interesting similarity between these two mythologies is that Ereshkigal is sometimes referred to as "Irkalla", an alternative name of the land of the dead, or the underworld. When used in this manner, her name appears to be similar to that of Hades, where, as mentioned, is the name for the God of the Underworld as well as being a name for the Greek Underworld itself.

I realize that all of this background information about Ereshkigal may still not initially connect her to being connected with healing, however the myth of "The Descent of the Goddess" is one that commonly forms the backdrop when undertaking shadow work. Being aware of this additional information about Ereshkigal, I started to wonder whether this would also reveal a difference in my own healing work. Instead of perceiving her as merely an antagonist to Inanna, what would connecting with the ruler of the Great Below reveal? It was this alternate approach that brought about a rather unexpected connection with this Underworldly Goddess that paved the way for a level of personal healing, not to mention insight, that I had not expected.

Before I go any further, I should remind the reader that there are many tools and techniques available that enable healing to be undertaken, especially when deeper emotional and psychological traumatic wounds are being considered. The end result that can be achieved often depends on how deep you wish to submerge yourself in your pain, especially that which has long roots stemming back into the past. There will also be times when one method or technique can only take you so far, and then you find that another is needed to render the desired result. I say this because healing, especially at a deep soul level, can take a great deal of time. It will often involve a lot of patience, not to mention courage, especially if there are many layers needing to be exposed and dealt with before the true root cause, originating issue, is exposed. I have also found that you need to allow a deal of flexibility, openness and even acceptance (trust) because what you may initially have considered to be the source of all your pain, may in fact actually be covering a deeper issue that has long been forgotten about.

Allowing ourselves the time and space to explore the deeper, underlying sources of our pain, not to mention the integration that is needed afterwards, are also important factors to keep in mind. In truth, as there is so much unresolved trauma contained within our world today, this mere thought could send you into states of overwhelm. Yet, when you apply the various tools and techniques available, or what resonates with you, healing too can flow out into the world as perceptions of the past change and an increasing number of people open themselves up to a new way of projecting into the future.

A further point of note is more of a reminder in that when it comes to deep soul healing it can very well come to us from rather unexpected sources. This was certainly my experience as, much to my surprise, I discovered my guide through such deep healing emerged to be the formidable Ereshkigal. In spending time to outline the various myths that may not be familiar to all, I feel that these may actually assist the reader in looking at Ereshkigal in a different light, moving her beyond being perceived as only the ferocious antagonist to Inanna, not to mention somewhat disconnected with what is happening on the upper realms.

As I have mentioned earlier, while I had worked with "The Descent of the Goddess" myth when it came to shadow exploration, these experiences had been voluntarily. In 2015 things changed completely as this freedom of choice was taken out of my hands completely when I was diagnosed with a potentially life-threatening health condition, and found myself standing before the first gate to Ereshkigal's realm. Over the following weeks and months, I followed Inanna, step by step, as at each gate I was forced to relinquish an aspect of my identity, that of the self I had projected to the world, and the perceptions on what I had thought life had install for me. All the ego-centric moments I had built my life upon, often without any due thought, in relation to other people and not my own self, all began to slip away from me as I continued through each gate. In "The Descent of the Goddess", as indicated, through the last gate, naked and bent low, Inanna found herself before the mighty Ereshkigal. Exhausted from the intensive medical regime I was undertaking, not to mention the ego-centric attempts to keep up appearances that I was capable of looking after myself (too proud to ask for assistance as this would be a sign of weakness), the Queen of the Great Below enticed me further and further into her Underworld realm where I found, not a vengeful, frightening goddess, but one who openly welcomed the unmentionable pain and anguish that we so often attempt to absorb ourselves.

According to the myth, when Ereshkigal fastened her eye of death upon Inanna and spoke the words of wrath against her, the Queen of Heaven was hung on a hook for three days and three nights before the kurgarra and the galatur slipped into the Underworld. Here, they witnessed the suffering that Ereshkigal was going through, and stated to mirror her pain:

"Oh! Oh! My inside!"
"Oh! Oh! Your inside!"
"Oh! Oh! My outside!"
"Oh! Oh! Your outside!"

This display of empathy and compassion was so power that it stopped Ereshkigal in her grief. Indeed, the Dalai Lama has been reputed of saying that the only thing that equals the power of wisdom is that of compassion. In "The Descent of the Goddess" it is this act of compassion that enables Inanna to be released as the creatures desired to have the "corpse" as reward for the empathy they showed. In my own meeting with Ereshkigal, it was she who was the giver of compassion. Once through the final gate, I found myself in the presence before the ruler of Irkalla, the Underworld, the antagonist of the Queen of Heaven, the alleged vengeful one. Dare I look upon her face in the half-light? If I did, would I too find myself upon the hook, what was left of my existence, the life that I had known, nothing but an empty shell?

As I have mentioned, things are not always what they seem. Yes, in a way I did find myself on a hook and even a "corpse", yet this was a necessary period of rest, of simply being to enable the transformation that I was undertaking, at a deeper soul level, to take place. Such as process is often described as being likened to the transmutation that a caterpillar goes through in the chrysalis before emerging as a butterfly.

Or maybe it is likened to the alchemical transmutation of lead into gold. What is often overlooked is the actual dissolving of the first stage before the re-emergence of something new. Here in the Underworld, I was forced to simply be. Here in Irkalla, I was forced to dissolve all aspects of the ego-centric self that I had once identified with. Here in the shadowy realms of the Great Below, I was confronted with the need to dissolve the old in order to make way of the new.

My illness gave me an appropriate excuse to make a change in my life – that is, if I was brave enough to completely surrender. And this is the unexpected gift that Ereshkigal offers in her shadowy realms, the gift of simply being. The much-needed gift of integration when your world seems to be spinning out of control. The opportunity to become a spectator of your life, removed from all emotional attachments that can cloud your forward movement.

The Alchemical Process

When the caterpillar spins its chrysalis, it instinctively knows that in order for transformation to occur, the old life needs to be dissolved. This is likened to the Nigredo (black) stage within alchemy which involves the breaking down of the existing substance. Within our personal lives, this relates to the dissolution and chaos that we find rising to the surface when we begin to work with our unconscious or shadow. It is here that we face out internal demons, our inner dragon, through the melting of personal desires and aversions, the collapsing of identifications and even belief systems. All of this release, surrender, removal is essential in order for the process of transformation to occur. It is, after all, considered to be the stage of purification within alchemy. The result of the Nigredo stage is often feelings of confusion and lost however this breaking down is necessary in order for the next step in the progress to occur – that of Albedo, the whitening stage. Having stepped into Ereshkigal's realm, we also step in the Nigredo stage of deep soul healing.

During Albedo, clarity may begin to emerge as insight is can be gain into areas that may not have been revealed to us before. After the somewhat turbulence of the Nigredo phase, we may find ourselves in a position where we are able to look at things from a different perspective. We are able to do this because of the breaking down that occurred during Nigredo. I liken this stage to being hung on the hook, like Inanna where she was transformed into a corpse. The Albedo alchemical stage is where the only thing we can do is to surrender to the process that we are needing to undertake. After all, when things are happening on a deeper level, they are actually out of our hands, so we just have to let things be. The third alchemical stage is that of Citrinitas, or the yellow stage, which is heralded as the arrival of a higher state of awareness, deeper insight, and even heightened trusting of our intuition. As we gain a fresh sense of insight and comprehension into ourselves and our place within the greater scheme of things, we realise that we have moved beyond the ego-centric problems of our daily existence. It is within this stage that we begin to gain a deeper understanding of the significance of the turmoil and chaos that we have undertaken – seeing the light at the end of the tunnel so to speak. Within Inanna's descent, Citrinitas can be likened to the arrival of the kurgarra and the galatur, where through their actions of empathy towards Ereshkigal, they set in motion what is needed for Inanna's return to the Upper World.

The fourth and final state of the alchemical process is that of Rubedo, or the reddening stage. (red) stage to take place. This point is the zenith of the process, which is defined by the fusion of our conscious and unconscious selves. At this point, we may feel like our life finally has significance and we have found our true place in the world. We are transformed due to our experience and the journey that we have undertaken. This often results in a new self-understanding and set of goals. It also includes incorporating the knowledge acquired over the preceding steps. Once this realisation has taken place, we begin to act in accordance with our new core beliefs and innermost desires which may be in complete opposite to what we held previously. According to psychoanalysis Carl Jung, once the stage of Rubedo has been reached, it is the climax of the alchemical process as it represents the realisation of one's unique potential through the realisation of own self-awareness. This is because we have been able to transcend our own ego. When looking at this alchemical stage within the context of "The Descent of the Goddess", once having returned to the Upper World, Inanna then perceives her relationships in a different light, especially that of her consort Dumuzi.

What is very interesting about "The Descent of the Goddess" is while the main focus appears to focus on the Queen of Heaven, it is actually Ereshkigal and the role she plays in instigating the deeper alchemical journey, that is ultimately important. While this may not be evident when the focus is on Inanna, this realisation can certainly be found in the last few lines of the ancient poem:

"Holy Ereshkigal! Great is your renown!

"Holy Ereshkigal! I sing your praises!"

The realisation that I made is no matter how we utilise "The Descent of the Goddess", even if for voluntary shadow exploration, it is actually Ereshkigal, and not Inanna, who encourages us to this journey. It is into Ereshkigal's realm that we must descend. It is Ereshkigal who removes the distractions and excuses that we may hide behind in order to avoid undertaking the deeper soul work that is needed to heal ourselves. It is Ereshkigal who then provides the space where we can submerge deep into the healing, allowing us to completely dissolve. And finally, it is Ereshkigal who continues to remind us, offering us strength and encouragement, as our fragile new self emerges back into the world again.

Connecting with Ereshkigal

Aside from utilising "The Descent of the Goddess" where Inanna's descent is reenacted as a means to enter into the shadowy realms of my own subconscious to ascertain what is hidden there, my connection with Ereshkigal, especially on a deeper healing level, occurred over ten years ago. I distinctly recall attending a visiting exhibition on the wonders of Mesopotamian artifacts when she "appeared" in my consciousness as almost a whisper, suggesting I need to look for the "truth". I left that exhibition with a number of more scholarly works that I probably would not have normally been exposed to, and as I started to read them, I realized that this "truth" was about who she truly was, beyond the modern interpretation (at the time) of her.

As my own practice in connecting with deity is through researching their myth in order to construct a suitable altar, ritual and meditation, she next appeared during a ritual that focused around her younger consort, Nergal, the God of Pestilence and War, where his martial attributes were the focus.

On this occasion she was a shadowy presence who appeared in an underground chamber attempting to entice me to cross the abyss into her realm.

Despite working with darker forms of deities, including those who are rather chthonic in nature, my encounter with the ruler of the Great Below was through my illness as I have outlined, albeit somewhat briefly, above. However, it was the emergence from the Great Below, from my Rubedo state that continues, each time cycling back into the Underworld to rest, release, transform before emerging again. This endless process is almost a constant reminder of that life is but one small part of the larger endless cycle that includes birth, death and rebirth.

Branwen, Healer of Hearts

Tiffany Lazic

There is a tale I tell on rare occasions. It is a wrenching tale in many ways but one that, for me, activates the true nature of wonder and brings to life a sense of the tangible, engaged relationship to the Divine to which we are all privy.

By the age of 19, my son had been struggling for several years. I can pinpoint the beginning of the downward spiral three years earlier when, out of the blue, he received a phone call from his estranged biological father who then sank down into the mists again. No amount of guidance, support, or counselling seemed to touch the pain that was complicated by all the additional earmark challenges that come with moving solidly into adolescence. Distressingly, but perhaps unsurprisingly, drugs became part of the equation. And then very terrifying moments of aggression and breaks with reality began to appear. At the very worst of it, when I found my son locked in a bathroom screaming that he wanted to die, I made the terrible call to the police to have him taken to the hospital for involuntary admission.

For much of this years long journey with my son, I held the Goddess Rhiannon close by my side. I had met Rhiannon, along with several other Welsh Goddesses, when I became a member of the Sisterhood of Avalon in 2007. She appears in *The Mabinogi*, a collection of Welsh tales found in two primary medieval sources, Llyfr Gwyn Rhydderch (The White Book of Rhydderch c. 1350 and Llyfr Coch Hergest (The Red Book of Hergest c. 1382 – 1410), although the origin of the stories is said to date much earlier. Though there are other stories that appear in the two medieval manuscripts and not every story appears in them both, *The Mabinogi* is unique in its seeming cohesive thread of storyline, presented as four tales, or more precisely, four branches. Rhiannon appears in the First Branch (Pwyll, Prince of Dyfed) as an Otherworldly being who chooses to live in the mortal world as the wife of Pwyll. Upon the birth and mysterious loss of their firstborn, She is accused of murder and set a shaming punishment which She endures for many years, though She knows Her innocence. At the end of the tale, Her son is restored, the truth prevails, and Rhiannon reclaims Her rightful place. The tragedy that befalls Rhiannon seems all the more so because of Her Otherworldly nature and Her choice to live in the mortal world. Her endurance of Her trials seems to speak even more highly of Her dignity and grace under inordinate pressure. Developing a relationship with Rhiannon taught me to pay attention to those times when I needed to reach out for help, to remember that circumstances do not determine my worth, and that, as hard as this human life can be at times, at my heart I believe I chose to be here and experience it. There is great power and great comfort in that reflection, but it was the Third Branch that had an even more profound effect on me.

In the Third Branch (Manawydan, Son of Llŷr), Rhiannon's son, Pryderi, now grown, married, and Lord of Dyfed after his father, returns from a terrible war with Ireland (that figures in the Second Branch). Of the very few warriors who lived to return to Wales, one is Manawydan who marries Rhiannon, thus becoming Pryderi's step-father. There are threads unfolding from even before Pryderi's birth which snake disruptively into the lives of these four, Rhiannon and Manawydan, Pryderi and his wife Cigfa, bringing trials of entrapment and illusion. In the second trial they encounter, Pryderi, ignoring Manawydan's advice, enters a mysterious castle and touches a golden bowl suspended over a well, becoming stuck fast. Rhiannon discovers him there and tries to help him but ends up becoming stuck fast herself. It is much later in the tale that Manawydan discovers the source of the enchantment and restores the two to the known world again. In the place where I was in my own life watching my son's struggles, it felt like clear advice on the trap of enmeshment when it comes to dealing with addiction. As contrary to every innate mother's instinct that was quivering, Rhiannon showed me that if I became ensnared in my son's struggles, we would both be lost. Instead, I tried to follow Manawydan's example of maintaining the course while paying attention to what was really going on under the surface. Ultimately Manawydan discovers that all the trials and illusions had been caused by a friend of the one Rhiannon had rejected in order to marry Pwyll. Bringing the truth to light and holding fast to his discernment and wisdom, Manawydan is able to bring the world back to rights again.

In navigating a challenging course through turbulent waters with mythic guidance, seeing my son with his hand stuck to an enticing but illusory cauldron, I tried to focus on maintaining the needs of my own life while at the same time trying to support him with compassionate inquiry into underlying causes of mental and emotional distress and facilitating access to professional resources. All of which resulted in my son's weeklong hospitalization in the psychiatric ward of the hospital with a discharge plan that included medication and access to group therapy on an outpatient basis. Which all seemed very hopeful. Unfortunately, the week between hospital discharge and the start of the outpatient program was horrific. A week in a facility is not enough to anchor any significant changes. My son returned to substance use which, when mixed with his prescribed medication, was disastrous. I tried to engage and support him, all the while reaching for Rhiannon for my own guidance and support, but I felt my grasp towards Her kept slipping. I wanted help in how to endure, but endurance requires the energy of hope and there were aspects of hopelessness that seemed to be appearing in the situation. Things out of my hands. It was during this time, for the first time in my years with the Sisterhood and study of *The Mabinogi*, that I began to reach out to another Goddess, one whose story had been far too painful for me to really dive into with any depth, one I had always kept at arm's length. But, in these acutely painful days, it was Branwen who called to me.

Branwen's devastating tale is told in the Second Branch (Branwen, Daughter of Llŷr). Sister to King of Britain, Bendigeidfran (Bran the Blessed), her doomed marriage to Matholwch, King of Ireland results to a horrific war. The impact of her treatment is referenced in Triad 53 of The Welsh Triads (also found in the Llyfr Coch Hergest)

Three Harmful Blows of the Island of Britain:

> *The first of them Matholwch the Irishman struck upon Branwen, Daughter of Llyr; The second Gwenhwyfach struck upon Gwenhwyfar: and for that cause there took place afterwards the Action of the Battle of Camlann; And the third Golydan the Poet struck upon Cadwaladr the Blessed.*

There are many, many layers to Branwen's tale, as there are with all of those in *The Mabinogi*. But there are two particular aspects to it which always made it achingly difficult for me to access. One was it read for me like a horror story that keeps getting relentlessly worse and worse. Each new piece to the story winds the tragedy ever tighter until you feel it is clawing its way slowly to a bitter, hopeless end, generally through the actions of Branwen's half-brother, Efnisien, whose very name means "strife". Any attempt to find a solution to impasse is thwarted by Efnisien, until the only option is war. And it is apocalyptic. All the Irish warriors die. All that remain are five pregnant women who are the ones to repopulate Ireland. Every warrior who comes from Britain to save Branwen, except for seven, all die. This includes Her beloved brother, Bran. In fact, and this is the second aspect I always struggled with in the story), it is the murder of Her child, Gwern, by Efnisien, thrown on the fire in the meeting hall when the Irish and the Britons came together to seek reconciliation for the wrongs against Her, that provides the explosion of the powder keg to the brewing tensions. Rhiannon may have become ensnared by trying to help Her son, but Branwen is powerless to save Hers. She could only stand by helplessly as everything and everyone she loves dies. And it proves too much for Her. Upon returning to Her homeland, Branwen dies of a broken heart. In a field near the north end of the island of Anglesey (Ynys Môn) lies a stone, cracked in half, that is called Bedd Branwen (Branwen's grave). It is said to be her heart cleaved in two from grief.

As the days leading up to the start of the outpatient program my son was scheduled to participate in drew closer, his behaviour became more and more erratic and aggressive. He came more distanced and unreachable. We moved ever so slowly towards the start of what I prayed would offer some guidance and help for him, but increasingly I found myself calling out to Branwen, for the first time ever.

"Dear Goddess, help me find courage when my heart is breaking. Help my heart find strength in spite of the dark of hopelessness. Help me find the love through the sharp edges of the pain. My heart aches that you could not help your son. Dear Goddess, please help me help mine."

In finding that prayer lodging itself in my heart, echoing through my tears whenever I found myself in a quiet moment, though there were not many of those, I realized that Branwen did not invite a call to action or a response to a situation. Not the way Rhiannon did. She simply invited me to drop to my knees and feel the ache of my broken heart, knowing that love is at the root of the ache and that love will always, eventually, find the path.

But it starts with the surrender to the ache. Those days leading up to the start of the outpatient program were the most trying of my life, I thought at the time. I was wrong.

Day one of the program came. It was a Wednesday. The day I held my open, free, morning Goddess Meditation at my healing centre. This was a beloved weekly highlight I had been hosting for several years. Every week, whoever was able to show up that week gathered in a circle. Sometimes we were just a few. Sometimes there were over twenty men and women who showed up. I would place my "Bowl of Goddesses" in the centre of the circle, made up of five different goddess oracles. It was quite something at well over 200 different goddess cards. Each week, one person would be invited to connect in with group energy, put their hand into the bowl and pull a Goddess card. It always floored me how the absolute perfect Goddess always showed up to meet us where we were at. It was an additional favourite tradition of mine to invite a new person to the group to be the one to pull the card, if there happened to be a new person that week. With everything that had been going on that past week, I was very much looking forward to the meditation. I always found the group very inspiring and, of course, there was always a helpful message or reflection from the meditation itself.

At home, it quickly became evident that things were going seriously awry, that "the hand was struck fast to the golden cauldron". Every attempt to ease obstacles to just getting to the hospital and stepping through that door for help were thwarted and more quickly than I could have ever anticipated, my son dropped the anvil of the non-negotiable with "I would rather be homeless than stay in this house. It will be a long time before you ever see my face again" and he walked out the door, leaving me shocked, stunned, speechless and bringing me, once more, devastatingly, to my knees. Feeling the desperation of Rhiannon who just wanted to pull her son's hand from that illusory cauldron and the ache of a heart cleaved in two, I reached for Branwen. I rocked with these two as the world shifted beneath my feet to something wholly unrecognizable. A world in which I had completely lost the very thing that was the most dear to my heart.

I don't know how long I was held there before I realized that, very soon, people would be gathering at my healing centre. As a drop in event, I had no way of letting people know if it needed to be cancelled. I contemplated rushing over and putting a sign on the door, but something in me also felt that connecting with the Goddess – with whichever Goddess showed up – was exactly what I needed. I took a deep breath. I gathered my things. I held myself very carefully. I felt like glass with a spiderweb of cracks. Held together by something tenuous, but at least holding together. And I went to open up my healing centre for the weekly Goddess Meditation.

This was one of those full weeks. My classroom was ringed with many familiar, dear faces and one unfamiliar one. A young woman who had never been before. I don't quite know what it was that kept me going in those moments, other than years of experience with bracketing (the ability to momentarily put aside deep emotional pain until an appropriate time to process) and group facilitation. I did share I had had a tough morning out of respect for the energy that I was bringing to the group, but other than that I tucked the pain to the side until I had the time and the privacy to look at it fully again. And, looking around the group to see who might want to pick the week's Goddess, my gaze landed on the unfamiliar face sitting right across from me, directly across the circle. I explained the tradition of having a new person pick the Goddess if they felt so called and invited her to do so. She stepped up to the bowl and took a lovely, peaceful moment, seeming to gather herself and then put her hand into the bowl of hundreds of oracle cards. She pulled one out and walked over, offering it to me.

Rhiannon

A jolt went through me. The chances of that particular card being pulled, on that day, given my prayers of less than an hour ago, say nothing of all the prayers that week. It was miraculous. I took the card from the woman, probably shaking a bit. And I realized I had not caught her name when we did the initial circle check in so I said, "I'm sorry. I didn't catch your name."

"Branwen", she said.

And the glass shattered. I can't tell you what happened next. I know somehow, I led a meditation. I know that what came to me in meditation was the message, loud and clear, "The Goddesses and Gods walk amongst you when you most need a reminder that miraculous is immanent". I know that, even though that night was the worst in my life, as I rode waves of grief that carried me into the depths of my loss, that were not all that unlike the waves of contractions that had carried me into the depths of my joy at my son's birth, I felt the Goddesses as my midwives. Rhiannon carrying me to surrender and Branwen holding my grieving heart. The day's events brought them to me in a way that felt non metaphoric but significantly tangible and they have stayed with me, these two. I have worked with many other energies, many other faces of the Divine, but Rhiannon and Branwen have been constant.

With all the grace in my heart, I wish I could reflect that, all these years later, it all worked out. That working with these Goddesses has brought me and my son to a happier, healthier, and more hopeful way of being in the world, free of addiction. That Manawydan found the underlying cause and freed us all from illusion. But, ever so sadly, that is not the case. Not all that unlike Branwen's tale, things got worse and worse. There would be a slight respite. The small opening of hope that the desire to challenge the addiction was holding enough strength to gain a positive foothold, and then something would happen to cause all the progress to come crashing down. Every time there was a small opening of hope, my son would reach out to me and I would be there immediately. There was never a closed door, but I knew he needed to take the step towards it, not me bring it to him. The hope, the healthy behaviours, the plans for the future would hold for a little while, and then the slide would start. Then the pulling away would show up and finally the full rejection and the cut off would happen. The final time going through all this which transpired through the whole global COVID journey was both the most painful to experience and filled with the most grace. Heartbreakingly and tragically, he did not survive it. At the age of 24, my son succumbed to addiction and took his own life. The grace is that he left the planet knowing he was loved. Knowing that he was cherished. Knowing that he was surrounded by a circle of support. The last words he ever heard from me were "I love you more than anything". The last message I ever received from him was "Beautiful mother I am proud of you".

Sometimes there are not happy endings. Branwen absolutely teaches us that. Bedd Branwen, the massive stone cracked in two, is a starkly beautiful reflection of that. Branwen showed me that you love regardless. You love in spite. You love because that is the only thing that really matters. And because your heart is stronger than the pain. Rhiannon can help you endure, and that is so important. But Branwen helps us to navigate the unendurable. And there is only one way through that. That is through love.

Aphrodite: Healing the Wounds of Abandonment
Becoming/Reclaiming Your Own Love Spell

Irisanya Moon

Immortal Aphrodite on your golden throne,
daughter of Zeus, wile-weaver, I beg you,
don't crush my spirit, queen,
with anguish and pain:1

I met Aphrodite reluctantly, then accidentally, then necessarily, after many years of avoiding her. It's not that I didn't want love or that I didn't long for beauty in my life, but I didn't want the mirror that Aphrodite seemed to offer. I wanted to stay far away from anything and anyone that offered love spells. Or the idea that I could be worthy of love without having to work as hard as I had been told I needed to.

I didn't want anything to do with a being whose ethos and reputation smelled of superficial longing and lusting. That was the magick of attraction, and it was easy, simple, and, well, boring to me. I was more interested in the deities who would put me through my paces, who would harden me further instead of softening. After all, softening was the work that would make me more susceptible to injury. To damage. To more damage.

I didn't want another important figure to crush me in ways I had not anticipated. I did not want to sign up for another connection that would eventually end in separation and abandonment – the kind of breaking that only comes when you were promised it never would.

but come here, if ever before,
hearing my cries from far away,
you left your father's golden house
and came here

I left my family for another side of the country because I could not expand my arms in the Midwest. I could only stretch wide enough to be noticed as something different, something strange, and something that couldn't claim itself fully. Leaving the golden house, the place of my beginning and my understanding that love could be something that was inconsistent and corruptible, was a necessary journey. A step forward that placed my feet on a land that would love me alive.

But only if I was brave enough to close my eyes. This was long before Aphrodite, and it was also the beginning of knowing how my hand would fit in hers. Because we shared stories that we would only recognize ten years later. She heard my cries or I heard hers. I'm not sure it matters when the voice began to echo in my head and heart. I'm not sure it matters if the sound was a scream or a sigh.

I knew it was pulling me to the place where love could put me back together, but it was not the love I'd made vows to. It was the love that had shattered inside of me the first time I realized my mother's smile was only the easiest of lies and my home was only a place to recognize as a point in my timeline. A place I would see out of the corner of my eye when I decided to look back at all.

It was the place where my then relative-by-marriage seemed to approach death in her grief the moment the truck was ready to pull away. That city was the waves of leaving because that's what you do when you are the tide and gravity does what it does. The leaving was always going to happen, and it's better when you leave because you want to. Because you need to.

with your chariot yoked, and beautiful
quick-winged birds led you over the dark earth,
fluttering their fast wings down from heaven
through midair.

There is a part of leaving that allows you to know the magick, to know what is possible in the unknown. I can tell you long stories of how I couldn't catch my breath, how I saw dragonflies everywhere, how I felt my heart expand and open, and how I knew this was all going to end with a decision I would not be strong enough to make. Yet.

The open road didn't tell me any of this. I recognized what was coming the second I said I would support whatever came next, no matter what. I knew I was lying, though I had been taught this selfless lie was the kindest one you could tell. And I had been told it so many times, it felt more like a greeting or the 'how are you' that no one actually wants the answer to.

I said I would go to the very end, to the stars, to the magick of surrendering everything for love for you. I know now how this was the cruelest promise I could make to you. And it was all I could think to say (and believe) when I was afraid of being alone. Of being un-worshipped. Of being un-tended. Of being abandoned.

The abandonment wound is the wound of unworthiness, caused when your caregiver did not show up for you in the ways that you needed. You did not get the attention you asked for and the attention you deserved. This may not have done this purposefully, but the lack of connection creates a deep void and a deep cavern that knows only its emptiness. And will do anything to not feel the spaciousness and silence. All you needed was to be yoked to something steady – and it never came.

This wound arrives as something confusing and inconsistent. I recognized it in the way I was never sure if my parents loved me from day to day. I could assume it, but it wasn't shown or seen or felt. Each day, I woke up feeling like I needed to prove myself again, and hopefully know my worthiness in their eyes. (I think being a Catholic made this an easy thought process. For that god seemed to love when you were loveable and docile. When you were the 'right' version of good.)

We can feel abandoned when they walk away, when they turn away, when they die, or when they just don't show up when we really, really need them. When no one else will do. And we are left with the idea this is normal, that something is wrong with us because if a caregiver or parent can leave us, anyone can. This abandonment is somehow right and it is what we should expect from anyone who might love us. Who might dare to love us.

And we will say anything ANYTHING to not be alone. To chase after those who are running away from us. To give and give until we have scraped the bottom of the heart and beyond. To pretend everything is okay even when living feels like dying. While those we love are not our parents, they are also supposed to love us and tell us what to eat and remind us that we are loved and that they noticed we needed to eat in the first place, right?

Aphrodite knows abandonment intimately and publicly. When the beautiful human, Psyche, shows up, everyone wants to meet her and worship her instead.

A.S. Kline's translation of *The Golden Ass* describes the abandonment of Aphrodite:

> Crowds of eager citizens, and visitors alike, drawn by tales of this peerless vision, stood dumbfounded, marvelling at her exceptional loveliness, pressing thumb and forefinger together and touching them to their lips, and bowing their heads towards her [Psyche] in pious prayer as if she were truly the goddess Venus. Soon the news spread through

neighbouring cities, and the lands beyond its borders, that the goddess herself, born from the blue depths of the sea, emerging in spray from the foaming waves, was now gracing the earth in various places, appearing in many a mortal gathering or, if not that, then earth not ocean had given rise to a new creation, a new celestial emanation, another Venus, and as yet a virgin flower.

Day by day rumour gathered pace, and the fame of her beauty spread through the nearby islands, the mainland, and all but a few of the provinces. People journeyed from far countries, and sailed the deep sea in swelling throngs, to witness the sight of the age. Venus's shrines in Paphos, Cnidos, and even Cythera itself were no longer their destinations. Her rites were neglected, her temples abandoned, her cushions were trodden underfoot, the ceremonies uncelebrated, the statues un-garlanded, the altars cold with forsaken ashes. The girl it was, that people worshipped, seeking to propitiate the goddess' great power in a human face. When she walked out of a morning, they would invoke transcendent Venus in feast and sacrifice. And as she passed through the streets, crowds would shower her with garlands and flowers.

She who *is* beauty is forgotten; her shrines left untended. Her name falling away from people's mouths as their eyes turned to Psyche. Aphrodite is not worshipped as she once was, as she knows she should be. And she longs to be remembered and celebrated. Understandably, Aphrodite is angry, furious, and vengeful. She wants to make Psyche know her pain.

Aphrodite sets challenges on Psyche, from a husband Psyche is not allowed to see to impossible tasks that take her to the River Styx and nearly to her death.

For just a moment, Aphrodite forgets who she is: Love. And she seems to forget that Love is not something that can be forgotten.

Soon they arrived, and you, blessed one,
with a smile on your immortal face,
asked me what had happened now and
why I had called you

I called to Aphrodite when I knew I was ready to know Love. Now, I have been in love many times, sometimes unrequited, sometimes in full agreement with another. I know the tingles and the tangles of this connection. The ways love arrives as a smile you can't stop and the sleep you don't want anymore. In a sense, love feels like abandoning of all reason, and I invite it in my chambers whenever it can visit. But there was a new sensation that was starting to curl my toes. And it was the recognition that even as I showed up for love, I was showing up half-heartedly.

I was showing up a shadow and the shape of what I thought I needed to be. And Aphrodite will not change who she is, and she implores me to do the same. Show up in your full-bodied glory and grit. Show up as the brightest of smiles and the deepest of fears. Love can hold all of this at the same time. It does not abandon when things are hard or confusing. It sits down, listens, and holds your hand anyway.

Aphrodite's marriage to Hephaestus is the next abandonment, the time she stays in a marriage because it is arranged for her. She abandons the idea of love for the act of duty. And she continues to have affairs because she does not love her husband. She wants the passion and intensity she doesn't feel in her marriage. She wants what she wants, no matter what it looks like to others.

Healing the wound of abandonment begins here. It begins with knowing what you want and claiming it, even if it is hard and unpopular. But when you have been what everyone else wanted for so long, it is a long road to return to who you are.

It can feel uncomfortable, aggressive, and selfish. To truly see yourself without the impact or advice of another is the work.

You might think of it as one of Aphrodite's challenges to you and the way she can hold up a mirror. The reflection of all that you are. I knew she would ask me to gaze into my own eyes and remember. I would have to call myself worthy before I could claim anything more.

Mirroring Your True Desire

What you need:

mirror
journal, pen/pencil

Find a quiet space to sit. Get comfortable and call out to Aphrodite to be your guide in this work. You don't have to have a long invocation to her or anything special. You can simply touch your heart and ask her to be present with you.

Hold the mirror and look at your face. Look at the way you can look into your eyes and notice the way this might be uncomfortable. Know this is not a practice of judgement or assessment. This is a practice of giving yourself the attention that others have not given you. And the attention you may not be giving to yourself.

In the mirror, talk to yourself (aloud or in your head) about what you really desire and want in your life. This is the list of the things you really want: physically, emotionally, spiritually, sexually, etc. Take this time to sit with Aphrodite at your back and let all of your wants become visible. See how you look at yourself when you tell yourself what you really want from your life.

Let yourself list as many things as you like. Let all of the words and all of the wishes come out of you. This is not a time for dismissing anything you want or anything you have desired. This is a spell of seeing yourself for who you are.

When you feel you have said enough, you can stop and write down anything that surprised you. You can write down anything that you want to remember. You can take this list and put it on an altar to Aphrodite. You can let it be a petition that is sent to the godds. You can take these words into your own divine heart.

Thank Aphrodite when you are done. And you might ask her if you can remember desire and the holiness of desire every time you look in any mirror.

and what I wanted more than anything to happen
in my crazy heart. "Whom should I persuade now
to love you? Who, oh Sappho, is
doing you wrong?

Sappho is asked by Aphrodite if there is someone she loves, someone that Aphrodite could persuade to love the sweet poet. And Aphrodite asks what wrong this person has done.

The abandonment wound opens up each time there is a disconnect or perceived disconnect – when other seem to abandon temples they once visited regularly. Enter self-sabotage and pushing others away, showing ourselves and the world that we were always meant to be alone. See? We set challenges to those who love us, who genuinely love us. We question their motives and we hide what is true. We hide everything until we finally can't, and those who loved our falseness leave. Because they loved someone else, someone we tried so desperately to be.

Being abandoned and feeling unworthy of love is deep and unrelenting. It can make a person reach out for anyone who seems kind and caring. It can cause a person to be so self-sufficient that they never ask for help, as they trust no one to be there.

But this is a lonely life, one that is infused with the fear of being left again and again. In that terror, a person will abandon themselves. They will say yes to everything. They will change their hair, their appearance, their tastes, their personality, and more – all to ensure another person loves them. But this never works. Becoming a chameleon means you never see yourself or know yourself clearly. You forget who you are.

Aphrodite can hold complexity in those wide arms of love. As a deity who has been loved and lost, and eventually loved again, she knows where she comes from and who is to be trusted. She looks out for your heart and can be someone to turn to when you are in pain from those who have left. When you are in pain from feeling like you are always being left.

When my ex left, I took a picture of my face. It was late in the afternoon and I was tired and dissociated. I did not know this was happening on this particular day until it was happening. This may have been an intentional miscommunication or the hard slap of denial. I'm not sure, and I'm not sure I need to know now.

I sat on our bed. I leaned my head to the bedsheet and put a rhodochrosite necklace over my head; the string of stones was long enough to drop down onto my chest. I wanted to protect my heart. I wanted to protect myself from ever feeling the way I was feeling again. I turned to Aphrodite for protection. I turned to Aphrodite with the truth.

Confession Petals

What you will need:

A rose or other flower with many petals

Take some time to sit with yourself and get grounded in who you are. It will help to be in a place where you are undisturbed. Call again to Aphrodite in a way that feels right and true for you. Hold the flower in your hands and trace the surface with your fingertips. Let the flower be infused with your love and with the love of Aphrodite.

When Aphrodite asks Sappho who has done her wrong, it is the most genuine question. Seeing the poet in pain, the goddess asks why and who. Tell Aphrodite who has wronged you and how you have wronged yourself. Pull a petal from the flower and tell the goddess what has happened. What you have regretted. What you wish you would have done. How you have been hurt. How you have been abandoned.

Be angry. Be sad. Be disappointed. Be glad. Be grateful, or not. Be whatever you are. Just as you are.

Let all of the stories fall to the floor as you tell them. Each petal being the once beauty, now pieces of what was. Like a confession, let the words and feelings escape from you so that you might be healed. So that you might forgive others and yourself.

Forgiveness is not necessary, but sometimes it is the blessing you need. Sometimes forgiveness is the way to cut the cords that still attach us to the past. Forgiving ourselves can bring us back to this moment.

You can take these petals and throw them away. Or you can take them and use them in bath. This action can help to transmute what was harmful into what can now soothe. You can then let those waters run off of you and down the drain. Away away.

You don't have to hold onto anything you don't want to. You can, however, name what has hurt and make space for what will heal. Let that hurt be witnessed by yourself and by Aphrodite. Let what was once hidden away be seen.

For if she runs now, soon she'll follow,
and if she won't accept gifts, soon she'll give them,
and if she doesn't love now, soon she'll love you,
even reluctantly."

The abandonment wound is repairable, though the scar will remain a little lighter on your skin and easy to find. But scars can be so beautiful in certain lights. They can be reminders you trace your fingers over, like a smooth stone worn by water. What was rough can be caressed to softness, reminding the jagged that it is not forgotten or feared.

Love returns in other forms. It ignites the heart as the love spell of life, the love spell that you can remember the tune to when you are willing. When you are willing to step forward and onto the shore that is birth and becoming.

Abandonment might be the story of how someone didn't meet you when you needed to be met. But Aphrodite can teach us about how we can meet ourselves as easily. After all, when she did not have the love she wanted, she went out and found something else. She didn't wait around to have the love act in the way she thought it should.

Sometimes what is healing for us is not what others want it to look like. Healing can also be the small things no one sees or the bold actions no one understands.

Love Notes to the Self

Healing the abandonment wound begins with teaching ourselves that we can trust ourselves. That we will show up for what we need and the person we truly are. We will come forward each day to keep ourselves safe, to keep ourselves loved.

What you need:

Your list of desires/wants

This practice is about creating small rituals every day. There are many spiritual traditions that suggest a daily practice to help you have an anchor to yourself and the divine each day. These practices foster consistency of devotion, not only to divine, but also to self.

Show up for yourself, even if you don't think you are worthy of this attention. Especially when you don't think you deserve it. Your body needs to know you will not abandon yourself.

Take a look at the list of desires and wants from the previous practice. Choose one or two that are simple enough to do daily. The simpler they are, the better. You don't need to spend hours on this. In fact, it is best to choose something that is so easy, it doesn't really feel like it makes a difference.

But each day, do that thing. Do it every single day. The more you do this, the more your body and brain realize that when you say you're going to do something, you do it. You show up.

Show up for yourself every day to remember the love spell you already are. To remember that that universe called your name, and sang you into being.

> Come to me now, too, and free me from cruel
> cares, and do what my heart longs to
> see done, and you yourself
> be my ally.

You don't have to do this work alone. Just because you're healing a wound of everyone leaving (or the feeling that this is true), you can call out to others. You can learn to count on others. You can turn to a tree, a goddess, an ocean, or a song.

When I was about to fall apart, Aphrodite decided to make herself known. It was whispers and opportunities to meet her. It was her energy filling my bones and blood one night in a garden when I recognized I could be Love. Stepping out of myself, I created a vacuum of possibility and love rushed in and laughed. She told me I was already love. I was already the love spell I needed.

Because it's who I am. Because it's who everyone is. Because love is not a location or a person or even a feeling; love is a balm, it is a breath, and it is the connection of life. I avoided Aphrodite because I saw love in its imperfection, in its ability to abandon and to break. I saw love in how it could move in ways I couldn't predict.

But I spent so much time tracking love that I forgot how it moved when I laughed. How it sang when I wrote a poem about a bent branch or a white flower. I forgot that love was the reason I kept meeting the morning and the reason why I decided to get out of bed even when I thought no one would love me again. Love does not abandon because it is everywhere.

Love is the reason why my face looks different three years later. Why the pink stone necklace sits on an altar and not around my neck. Why the next picture I took shows how my eyes meet my own with the gaze of, "I will never leave you again."

Aphrodite is a divine being who has been abandoned by her devotees, by other deities, and by her lovers. Maybe it stems from (possibly) being born of the genitals of Uranus or being born in the Chaos of creation. Maybe having the mantle of being a deity of love and beauty is enough to create the need to be desired and connected at all times.

No matter the reason, Love is a story of leaving. Leaving what is easy, what is expected, and what we were once told is 'enough.' Love is reaching out for the hand that is already open, already willing, no matter what happens next. It is making the promise of stars and moon and all the way to the end because you mean it, not (just) because you want it to be true. It is making that promise because you know you will do all that you can until you can't anymore.

Not all temples will stay filled with the scent of worshipping. Not all shrines will hold relationships and connections that once knew the tone of your voice when you were scared. But love spells are everywhere. They are the whisper that you want more. They are the conversation you don't want to have. They are the poems you can write about sunlight as it travels from space to the edge of your bed through the blinds. Love spells are cast from the inside of you, even if the chambers are dusty and the chants haven't echoed off the walls in years.

You can reclaim yourself, make an ode to yourself. Remember your own sacred names. And call to Aphrodite if you ever forget again.

Keening with Brigit
Making Peace with Complex Grief

Mael Bridge

> Grief has become private, something to be contained, controlled. How very different in the time of keening when women were paid to cry, sing, and wail over the dead, to publicly display, articulate and channel the grief of a whole community.
>
> *Marie-Louise Muir, "Songs for the Dead"*

Introduction

This chapter is about three things: the grief of losing something precious (a friend, your health, etc.); complications of grief when betrayal or other conflict is involved; and how Brigit teaches us to acknowledge and proclaim our roots-deep pain, to use our voices to restore peace in ourselves. I'll talk about grief and betrayal in Brigit's life, and how my brother's death was made harder by my awareness of his suffering throughout life, and how I'd contributed to it.

Grief is seen in our society as something we need to get over. But it's a manifestation, a face, of love. Love can't exist without the possibility of grief.

We don't heal grief like a burn or cancer. We can't remove it; distancing ourselves from it distances us from love. Using our pain to beat up ourselves or someone else doesn't help. What we need to heal isn't our grief but our rejection of it. Far better to make peace with it, to become able to sit compassionately with whatever we find inside, whether anguish or numbness, affection or blame.

When grief is stifled by our thoughts and feelings, we can feel like a lifeless wasteland. Zen master Thich Nhat Hanh told a young nun,

> This space is very important. This is the ground, where everything will grow – the flowers, the grass, and the animals. You need to accept that this space exists inside you. Do not run away from it. Sometimes when the suffering is not in balance with the joy, you may feel the space as a vacuum. You may feel lifeless. Be there to embrace it. (healing, Sister Dang Nghiem)

When we turn to Brigit with our complicated sorrow, we find someone who faced her own complex grief head-on. She is a stable witness and guide.

Both Goddess and Saint Brigit have healing aspects. The goddess is three sisters: one each a patron of smiths, poets, and healers. Saint Brigit is called upon to protect and heal humans and animals, oversees many healing wells, and has areas of expertise, like aiding women in childbirth and treating eye ailments. But, although we may petition Brigit to aid in our recovery from the heart and body sickness that often come with grief, we won't focus on the healer. We seek the one who gives voice.

Morgan Daimler suggests that the Brigit of Cath Maige Tuiread, where we see her wounding, is the poet. In that story, she raises the first keen heard in Ireland. The Irish words used to describe it are those used for the "three demonic sounds after transgression in Ireland" that accompany "Brigit the poetess, daughter of the Dagda," in another text, the Lebor Gabala Erenn. Brigit exposing her grief this way echoes "Caoineadh Áirt Úi Laoghaire" ("The Lament for Art O'Leary"). His widow, Eibhlín Dubh Ní Chonaill, is said to have composed it where he lay murdered in 1773. It was known only in folk tradition until it was collected from one of the last professional keeners around 1800.

My Art,
I wouldn't give the time of day
to rumour of your death
until that selfsame mare of yours
came to me with her bridle awry,
her withers smattered
with your heart's damson,
and the polished saddle,
where I last saw you bolt upright,
lopsided and bereft.
from "Lament for Art O'Leary"
Eibhlín Dubh Ní Chonaill
Vona Groarke, trans.

Brigit's keen may not have been the sophisticated poetry of this lament, though perhaps it was. But it initiated, with its intensity of love and sorrow, a form that provided a vessel for the grief of Irish people for centuries, and which sometimes rose to a state of high art.

Brigit (and Vocalisation)

Brigit is an intricate being, known for centuries, who has transformed in our understanding over time. The saint has metamorphosed, then been blended into the goddess till it's difficult to know who is who. Little is known about the goddess, and it's uncertain whether any given Brig or Brigit in the early manuscripts is related to those who are daughters of the Dagda. Our tendency is to treat Brigit as one consistent, simplified saint/goddess with a perpetual flame and healing wells, who oversees the return of spring and the work of poets, smiths, and healers. But we can tease some strands apart for better understanding.

The clearest description of the goddess comes from Sanas Cormaic (Cormac's Glossary):

"Brigit – a poet, daughter of the Dagda. This Brigit is a woman of poetry (female poet) and is Brigit the Goddess worshipped by poets because her protection was very great and well known. This is why she is called a Goddess by poets. Her sisters were Brigit the woman of healing and Brigit the woman of smithcraft, Goddesses; they are three daughters of the Dagda..." (trans. by Morgan Daimler)

Brigit here is connected to high-status crafts and called on by their practitioners. There were other gods assigned the title of Smith, Physician, or Poet of Brigit's people, the Tuatha Dé Danann, but clearly, she shared those roles in some way, or at some locality and time.

The poets of ancient Ireland formed a social class equal to the king. They bore the knowledge of the people and could raise or lower one's fortune through well-aimed praise or satire. Smiths were half-magical persons who remained significant members of their communities until recent times. Healers were equally important, with high honour prices and many laws governing their conduct and responsibilities.

In the Lebor Gabala Erenn (Book of Invasions) we learn that the poet Brigit is associated with animals who are sovereigns of their own kind – kings of rams, boars, and cattle – supporting the idea that she is a sovereignty goddess, who is the land itself, conferring the power and authority to rule upon a deserving king, or withdrawing it if he proves himself unworthy.

In Cath Maige Tuired (Second Battle of Moytura), a rich and important work, we see a Brigit, daughter of the Dagda, mourning her son.

In all of these texts she is associated with vocalisation, whether of words or howls.

There is another group of three Brigits in the texts, who are connected to the great lawmaker, Senchae mac Ailella. They are his mother, wife, and daughter, but there is confusion around them as their titles can be interchanged in different manuscripts. They are his mother, Brig Briugu (Brig the Hospitaller), who must be a woman of great wealth to offer hospitality to all higher-class travellers, his wife, Brig Brethach (Brig of the Judgments), and his daughter Brig Ambue (Brig of the Cowless) who appears to represent "the fían or association of propertiless (literally cowless) and predominantly young, unmarried warrior-hunters on the fringes of settled society," (Kim McCone). Unlike Saint Brigit, who we see defending oppressed women, Brig Brethach is famous for her wise judgement regarding the rights of freeborn women of property. Her speaking out against her husband's error in this arena is another instance of vocalisation.

Saint Brigit has far more literature and abundant folklore related to her. The earliest writings are from the seventh century; they continue through the mediaeval period into modern times. Known for her fairness and generosity, particularly to the poor, she ushers in springtime and hope of survival to people dependent on the land and waters. Her feast-day, Fhéile Bhríde (Festival of Brigit) or Imbolc, is celebrated from dusk 31st January to 1st February. In earlier times, folk celebrated with simple feasts and prayers for protection, welcoming Brigit to enter and bless their homes. They took stock of their remaining food-stores and prepared for the coming season of fishing and farming.

The saint is independent, strong-minded, associated with healing and childbirth, and has many wells dedicated to her. She is a protector of the powerless, and her perpetual flame is tended by her nuns. As goddess, Brigit is patron of poets, smiths, and healers, provider of justice for women, hospitality to nobles, and care of young warriors on the fringes of society. Her attributes combine with the saint's to give us the Brigit we know today. We can't imagine the goddess without including the saint's characteristics, and vice versa. If they weren't linked in ancient times, they are intimately so today, and this rich combination makes her an especially dynamic deity.

Wounding

Brigit knows pain. In her understanding of many kinds of suffering, she can offer help to those who hurt. As goddess, as saint, she is there, steady and strong.

There are many examples of Brigit's response to wounding in the old texts.

Saint Brigit responded compassionately to the poor, sick, hungry and "mad," to humans and animals, such as the woman who was set up to lose her liberty by a man who wanted her as a sex slave, or the wild boar she rescued from hunters. She endured enslavement – her own and her mother's. In adulthood, she rescued various socially vulnerable individuals from powerful people who would harm them. One of these was her mother, still enslaved, who she travelled far to visit. Finding her ill, Brigit took over her work, and eventually won her freedom.

As a female she couldn't choose her course in life. In response to her brothers bullying her to marry when she was determined to become a nun, she plunged her finger in her eye, destroying her beauty and shocking them into trying to staunch her bleeding. The pain this caused her isn't mentioned, but it must have been considerable. In each of these tales is an intimate knowledge of hardship.

The goddesses Brigit come from a wealthy and dominant class and don't show the same affliction Saint Brigit experienced and witnessed. But that Brig Brethach corrected a false law set by her (usually wise) husband, to protect the property rights of women of higher classes – who had far less power than men – indicates her awareness of injustice. Brigit, healer and daughter of the Dagda, must have witnessed much suffering. Her poet sister, with her animal companions – two kings of the oxen, king of the boars, and king of the rams – feels and responds to the very wounds of Ireland:

"And with her were heard the three demonic sounds after transgression in Ireland, whistling and weeping and lamentation." (Lebor Gabala Erenn, trans. Morgan Daimler)

But it's the injury of the Dagda's daughter, likely the poet above, when she loses her son and raises her voice to keen, that we will look at. It is Brigit's most direct and harrowing wounding.

In Cath Maige Tuired, Brigit's husband, Bres, is made king of her people. Half Tuatha Dé Danann and half Fomorian, he is beautiful, excellent, a good replacement for the previous king. Yet Bres proves so stingy and cruel that even the land aches. A poet satirises him – one of the worst things that can happen – and he is deposed. War is the inevitable result, as Bres turns to his father's people, the Fomorians to help him seize back the kingship. Brigit and Bres's son, Ruadán, secretly sides with his father against the Tuatha Dé Danann. He tries to kill Goibniu, their smith, and is mortally wounded by him instead. Ruadán is taken to the Fomorian assembly, dying in front of Bres. When Brigit hears of it she goes to their camp, to her son's body. The impact of seeing him is so immense that she unleashes the first keen, a desolate, singing wail that became a part of Irish funerals for centuries to come, giving the bereaved a powerful ritual to hold and express their grief.

"125. Rúadán turned around after he was given the spear and wounded Goibhniu. He drew out the spear and cast it at Rúadán, it flew through him and he died of it in front of his father in the assembly of the Fomorians. Brighid came and keened her son. She screamed loudly and finally wept. This was the first time weeping and loud screaming were heard in Ireland." (Cath Maige Tuired, Morgan Daimler)

Death of Ruadán
withdraw sweet Brig
to the sunlit sídhe
happy place where death
is never known

feed yourself on apples
rest beneath the singing trees

your son is dead
your spirit trampled
when he threw the faithless spear
against his kin

Complicated Grief

Our grief may not be witnessed by our enemies or influence our culture the way Brigit's did. But when it strikes, it can alter our lives irrevocably.

I can attest to the devastating nature of bereavement, when the person who has died is so dear that their loss shocks us into feeling as if our limbs, our minds, our ability to go on living, vanished with their last breath. Such grief connects into every other deep loss of our lives, so that it can seem that there's no end to pain. When it's complicated by betrayal or other factors, it's even harder to endure; our mourning may be seriously impeded.

My brother Victor death two years ago devastated me. My grief is complicated, messy.

After the first months, when I was profoundly shaken and cried frequently, I found myself becoming remote from my grief. I could see it was affecting me: I felt dull, shut down, and when I tried to talk about Vic, detached: not in the sense that I didn't care, but I couldn't connect to feelings I knew were there. Sometimes I could feel, but couldn't cry.

I discovered that a hospice society had walks where participants could talk with others in the same situation. Those walks were so helpful. I wasn't alone in how I felt and didn't have to hold back, either to shield family or keep friends from feeling uncomfortable. But I still couldn't cry. Eventually I saw a bereavement counsellor, who I felt safe enough with that I cried deeply, gained some insights, and moved slowly toward peace. I'm still on that journey.

When I grieved Vic's death, both during his illness and after he died, I was overwhelmed with sorrow over his hard life, particularly as it had led to the illness that killed him. I could see, too, that my own struggles, as someone close to him, had contributed to his original wound and all that arose from it. His cares wouldn't have been so great if we, the family who cherished him, had been able to welcome him to the world without trauma, the personal and generational trauma that we ourselves endured. We were all older than him, and in fighting against the distress in our lives, we demonstrated an in many ways fraught and lonely world. He saw us in trouble and couldn't help. This was a burden he carried all his life.

Contemplating my role in his injury was so painful. Immersed in that pain, I saw wounds I'd received as a child: that the world wasn't as it should be. There was injustice, and I wasn't safe. My good treatment was conditional. And the world outside family largely saw me as too different. Unacceptable.

My gentle, good-humoured baby brother, whose greatest wish was for everyone to be kind to one another, counteracted this wound in ways I didn't realise. He never doubted my goodness. I always "fit in" with him. It became clear during his illness how important a role he'd played in my life by always liking and trusting me. His faith helped me see myself as more than a troublemaker, a weirdo; I was someone who saw injustice, someone worthy of trust, even admiration, and love. I trusted him entirely. Losing him, and that place of safety with him, was terrifying.

Love opens the door to grief. And even complex grief, when held with compassion, opens the door to forgiveness, self-forgiveness, and still greater love. If our families are instruments of our suffering, they inherited it from their families, their communities, in a thousand ways. It's only by finding ways to stop passing trauma along that I can heal – and help to heal my world. Facing my least favourite feelings kindly, so that I can mourn my brother in peace, is one way to do that.

We can look to Brigit, who entered into devastating grief and allowed its fullness to be expressed. With that cataclysmic expression, those "sounds after transgression," she changed her world. We can change our worlds by embracing all of our pain and all of our love. This doesn't mean acting them out thoughtlessly, or aiming that pain at ourselves or someone else. In a situation where everyone else was acting with violence, Brigit did not. Instead, she used the power of her grief and the trauma of her son's treachery and her husband's, to show the world the result of their misdeeds, to reinforce her love for Ruadán, and to allow her heart to break open completely. She thus gave her people a means to grapple with their own broken hearts.

Let's learn from Brigit how to give our grief, and all of its complications, the voice it needs to find peace. In claiming our voices, let's encourage those around us who remain unable to care for their heartache and claim their right to let it sing.

Brigit's Story and Mine

Having also tasted betrayal, I can imagine myself in Brigit's place and guess her pain. But as I explore my wound and hers, my perspective shifts. I began by identifying with Brigit's loss of her son. But her wound didn't begin with his death, or his betrayal of the Tuatha Dé; it began with Bres's ill-treatment of her people. Did she agonise as Bres's rule decayed, as Ruadán's disloyalty grew? Did she know something terrible was approaching?

In my case, what I want to make peace with is that I failed my brother – or in less accusatory words, couldn't offer him the quietude and security he needed to thrive. Along with sorrow for his hardship, hidden self-reproach has complicated my grief.

Still, Brigit's multilayered grief reminded me of my sorrow over losing Vic. Then I became aware of Ruadán's betrayal by his paternal kin, who used him cold-bloodedly.

How confused he may have been by his father's actions, and conflicted by a war between his own and his paternal grandfather's people. How had Ruadán chosen? What did it cost him emotionally? Did it change how he saw himself? What broke in him even before he threw the spear?

This unfurling spiral of perspectives make it difficult to stay with one view of Brigit's story or my own. I've gone from being Brigit to Ruadán, to Brigit again. I share her sorrow and his confused destructiveness; I feel the sorrow for my own destructiveness that he might have felt, had he survived. Although I never made war against my people, I grieve that my wounds led me to act from pain and hurt those around me.

I know I didn't cause my brother's cancer. I know that Ruadán didn't start the war. We're not told what kind of mother Brigit was, what relationship she and her son shared. But as a goddess of poets and poetry, she gave voice to a complex sorrow never lent such outcry before.

Writing this chapter has helped me remember that I didn't betray my brother. I was the best sister and friend to him that I was able to be, at every moment in our lives, even though I couldn't prevent his anguish. We were both betrayed – by the harms sustained from society against our forebears and ourselves, through class, religion, separation from family, and, in several generations, poverty and institutionalisation. By the stealing of children from a destitute mother, and a lifetime of workhouses for her because her husband had died; childhoods spent in "industrial schools," from which age or death were the only escape. The alcoholism that was one result of such torment, or the anger that never found peace. A grandmother living in a convent from early childhood, working for her board from four years old, again for the crime of poverty. The sense of having no value, no right to speak, being wrong in all our manners, of being the opposite of the so-called great and good. My siblings and I may never have entered a workhouse, but our inheritance was real, and clear to those who would use it against us.

Although Saint Brigit might understand this type of suffering, it's nothing the goddess, in her high-status family, would have known. But if I tell her, she'll listen.

For most of my adult life, unlike my childhood, I've borne my wounds in relative silence. Perhaps in writing this I'm borrowing Brigit's strength to vocalise the depth of my loss. In articulating my grief, I borrow her voice, and cultivate peace.

Making Sound

Vocalisations such as shouts, whistles, and so on have magical associations in Irish mythology, for instance the Lia Fáil (Stone of Destiny), which cried out when the rightful king stood or sat upon it. Poets' utterances could topple or elevate a king. Both the goddess and Saint Brigit have a connection to vocal expression, something extremely important for women in particular.

Once a supporter of Saint Brigit's visited, bringing her adolescent daughter, who'd been mute from birth. Brigit, not realising this, took her by the hand and asked whether she wanted to take the veil or be married. When her mother said she couldn't answer, Brigit replied that she wouldn't let go of her hand till she spoke. She repeated her question: the girl was able to answer and, from then on, speak without impediment.

So, where the goddess gives voice to her own distress and that of the land, the saint enabled another to speak.

As girls, women, and femmes, we have been silenced in countless ways for many centuries. Although as a collective women have been claiming our voices and are now heard in most arenas of life, it's still difficult for many of us to communicate our most painful experiences and feelings – say if we've been harmed or oppressed – and demand change in another or society. Great pressure against hearing our concerns persists. Brigit offers us a door into self-compassion and reclaiming our voice.

Brigit teaches us to use sound to protect our community from plunder by inventing a whistle for use at night when danger comes near. Her "demonic" sounds are unleashed after transgression. She doesn't hold back her grief, but wails and shrieks. She uses sound to express, proclaim, heal, and warn. These elements together suggest again her role as sovereignty goddess. The goddess who is the land itself is married to the king and her king has created havoc and sorrow. In response, the goddess protests.

She is also using sound on a personal level. She raises her voice, connecting deeply and without restraint to her loss, her wound, and all the shades of thought entangled in it. She declares her grief, ritualises it, and begins the journey toward making peace with it. At the same time, she is formalising the expression of grief by inventing the keen.

This brings to mind the work being done among First Nations in Canada and the U.S.A. around missing and murdered indigenous women, girls, and two-spirited people. By bringing their private grief and outrage into the public realm, they are marking the wrongs done to their communities and demanding justice. Perhaps there is something of this in Brigit's creation of keening, this public outcry. Perhaps she, too, is saying, "Look at this damage. Look at this loss. Look at the destruction of my child and ask yourself, 'What have we done? How will we reconcile with our community?'"

Within our complex grief, there may be elements of injustice, and in time we may need to publicly express our sorrow and outrage. It may be the loss of a loved one due to an opiate crisis created by pharmaceutical companies and supported by so-called "tough on crime" laws, criminalising people who are ill, driving those grappling with addiction, a medical condition, into crime or suicide. It may be seeing our natural world destroyed, and the terrible events occurring as a result of climate change. It may be grief rooted in economic injustice, poverty, and racism. Or perhaps we don't have the health or the heart or need to take a public stand, but we, too, need to express, ritualise, and begin making peace with our sorrow.

Opening the voice, to whatever degree is right for us, is one element of, and can sometimes lead to, opening the heart. But, allowing ourselves to give voice doesn't mean we have to do it; it means we are no longer barred from speaking, no longer barred from our own hearts. When we truly give ourselves permission to claim our voice, to no longer hide from ourselves, we may not feel the urge to make a sound, but what we do feel is relief and well-being.

t can take a long time to get to a place where we can open our heart and our voice with ease. It usually happens in increments over time. Either way, ritually opening our voice signals to our unconscious that we aren't limiting ourselves in this way anymore. That is the goal.

Additionally, making noise doesn't equal giving voice. We can scream and shout without ever accessing our deeper emotions and the truth we need to convey. This can be lonely and discouraging. Go gently, welcoming what wants to come and never trying to force an opening.

What Is Keening?

"Brighid came and keened her son. She screamed loudly and finally wept. This was the first time weeping and loud screaming were heard in Ireland." (Cath Maige Tuired, Morgan Daimler)

As it's written here, Brigit's keening doesn't seem to involve music or poetry. But what's known as keening in Ireland, a tradition that has only recently disappeared, is much more formal and elaborate. From Eibhlín Dubh's lament for her murdered husband to hired keeners at funerals, the keen ("sung lament" or caoineadh in Irish) was "the ritualised lamenting of the dead at a wake or funeral, in which the grief of the bereaved is expressed in song…" (JoeHeaney.org)

Its formal public practice … is well-documented: lamentation over the corpse by the deceased's female relations, and/or by a woman hired for the purpose, during the three days of the wake and at the burial itself. However, it's thought that an entirely separate private caointeoireacht was also observed by the bereaved family, for whom it would have served the dual purpose of bringing the dead person to mind and of giving vent to their own deep feelings of sorrow … (JoeHeaney.org)

Not very long ago when a person died "keeners" attended at the wake, and they cried aloud in a sort of singing voice and recounted the good deeds of the dead person. As a rule there used to be twenty-one keeners at a funeral and they followed the hearse in threes "keening". (Duchas.ie)

Keening at funerals long ago (c. 50 years) [?]. Four women usually. Wept themselves hoarse. Nóra Bhán mhín, a woman in the parish (Tuosist) who lived from ceithearnach to ceithearnach1, had a very sweet voice and no funeral was considered good unless she was one of the keeners. Any of the women who had a stream of poetry would put words into the keening. (Duchas.ie)

The word "ceithearnach" is linked to foot-soldiers and outlaws, but according to Geraldine Moorkens Byrne, "The professional keeners also travelled from parish to parish, but ceithearnach may in this context simply mean the tradition whereby they keened the coffin from to house to church/church to grave; [and] equally implies someone without a settled home or established role."

The keening woman, who was "paid" generally in a very small, almost symbolic, way – a glass of whiskey, a pinch of snuff, a plate of food – would call on her personal grief to find the sorrow needed to help others access theirs. She might throw her arms down and address the corpse, telling him what a fine man he was, how loved and respected, and so forth. She used her own words, within a convention of melody and often used words and phrases.

Marie-Louise Muir, a broadcaster in Northern Ireland, explored the loss of keening in Ireland in the BBC Radio 4 documentary, "Songs for the Dead":

It shocked and surprised me how difficult I found listening to those archive recordings. To my ear ... they were off-note. That unsettled me. It's akin to nails being scraped down a blackboard. Every atom of your body cringes against it. You just recoil. You're recoiling from the horror of loss, but this music is incredible. It's expressing how you're feeling.

Having gone through [grief] with [the funeral of] my own father ... you're also strangely euphoric because you've gone through a lot. To be in a room where your father breathed his last breath, you've never experienced that before. Then everybody, your family, the community piles in on top of you for a Catholic wake. Pots of tea and sandwiches are brought in. There's almost this party atmosphere. Everybody's dropping by.

You're giddy with lack of sleep, with grief. Everything's upended because you're having a party but the main person isn't there. To bring keening into the middle of that must have felt like you were breaking some kind of trance. That was in a way why it was so harsh – it must have been hard to penetrate the grief. (Richard Fitzpatrick)

Keening, and simply embracing the experience of our most complicated grief, is aimed at breaching that trance and regaining the full nature of our love and loss and the acceptance that follows.

As for Brigit, Chris Thompson of the Story Archaeologists points out,

... as the creator of 'keening', she has taken on a central poetic role. I am sure you know well, the high status of keening and elegiac poetry in Ireland. It was also closely associated with women... that offers two reasons why she gets paired with demonic sounds in the Lebor Gabala Erenn ... the ancient significance of keening, poetry beyond words, has become demonic bellowing. Only the connection between keening and sorrow (transgression) has been remembered. (pers. comm.)

If Brigit delivered the first keen in Ireland, was hers a composition of melody and words, created on the site where her son lay dead? Did she recount the good deeds of his life, retell the manner of his death, did she curse those who caused it? She was, if Daimler's guess and Thompson's implication are correct, a goddess of poets. She would have been steeped in the forms and nuances of the poet's art, and poetry in that oral culture was delivered aloud, in song. How else would she have mourned her son's death than with voice and memory and declaration?

I suspect that there was something ritualistic in what she did. This wasn't the first war in Ireland; many had died before Ruadán. Others would have mourned. But there's something different here.

This caoineadh is a very sad sort of a thing. You know by listening to them you would feel like crying yourself supposing you weren't sorry at all. And it was a rule in the past in Ireland when anybody be dead, they used to get these women to get them to cry, and pay them. Some of them had very sad crying. Oh, it was awful... (Uncertain, "Songs for the Dead")

... It was powerful. I mean, it would take the heart out of you. That's the reason that they done it, just to make you weep and this bereavement that people – they have to go to [a therapist] for help to get over it. They got rid of it through this. That's what it was all about, I think. But when it was done well, it was beautiful ... Just to send them off on the journey and to cry. It was very important to them. (Maggie, Inis Mor, "Songs for the Dead")

Like all of us, I've lost loved ones. I know what grief is. I imagine myself in the room with the keener. The hush, the anticipation, and then her song gives voice to the grief. A song for the dead. So, yes, I do yearn for someone to articulate it for me, to sing it out in all its rawness and pain. Words for the living to cope with death. (Marie-Louise Muir, "Songs for the Dead")

It's not possible to re-create authentic, traditional Irish keening. Although in "... the Irish tradition at least, it's clear that there's no established keening 'text,' but that the singer simply improvises as feeling dictates," (JoeHeaney.org) there were airs and words that were improvised from, a cultural context and acceptance of this as a norm, that are no longer available. But we can use the idea of the keen to create our personal laments, and we can bring elements of the tradition into our families and communities, where possible, to assist each other in coping with death.

When I lost a dear companion several years ago, I did just that, though not with keening in mind. In ritual, his body laid out before me, I began to call out to Brigit words that I later wrote down and added to. Since then I have sung it at memorial services, and it's made its way into the toolkit of at least one death celebrant. Although composed for one person, with little alteration it's been a vehicle for others' grief. In a small way, finding my voice in grief became a gift to my community. So, although we no longer have the context for traditional keening, we can use the idea to create our own declarations of loss and love, and with imagination and courage, can aid our communities and our world.

Prayer for the Dead
dear Brigit
I lay my loved one down
a last time

he is three days dead
we have wailed and wept
we have sung and laughed
we have given thanks
we have cried out in anger

we have given thanks

bless my loved one on his journey
let his coracle be light and leaping
on the waves

salmon his companions
and the great whales
to guide him to his home

Further Resources

The Keening Wake http://www.keeningwake.com/

"The world's most accessible stress reliever," Sarah Keating (2020)
BBC Future. https://www.bbc.com/future/article/20200518-why-
singing-can-make-you-feel-better-in-lockdown

Contributors

Morgan Daimler is a witch who has been a polytheist since the early '90's, following a path inspired by the Irish Fairy Faith blended with neopagan witchcraft. Morgan teaches classes on Irish myth, fairies, and related subjects in the United States and internationally. Morgan has been published in multiple anthologies as well as in Witches and Pagans magazine, and Pagan Dawn magazine. She has written several dozen books, including *Fairies: A Guide to the Celtic Fair Folk* and *Pagan Portals – Aos Sidhe*, has self-published books of Old and Middle Irish language translations, has a high fantasy novel *Into Shadow*, and an urban fantasy/paranormal romance series called *Between the Worlds*.

Halo Quin (they/them) is a pagan author, storyteller, singer-songwriter, and a lifelong lover of magic with a PhD in Philosophy. They have been a witch since childhood, and are a devotee of the Faery Queen, a lover of the Welsh gods, and a sensual witch exploring the divine erotic and sacred nature of pleasure and beauty, to (re)enchant the world. With roots in Feri, Reclaiming Witchcraft, and Druidry, Halo's magic weaves together devotion, story, community ritual, and listening to the Fair Folk, in an animistic path with an embodied approach to the Craft. Their books include *Gods and Goddesses of Wales, Faeries, Folktales, and Spirits* and *Crimson Craft – Sexual Magic for the Solo Witch*. Find Halo's books, classes, and storytelling here: www.haloquin.net

Irisanya Moon (she/they) is an author, witch, international teacher, Aphrodite priestess, and Reclaiming initiate who has practiced magick for 20+ years. She has taught Reclaiming magick at witchcamps in the US, Canada, the UK, and Australia, bringing a blend of grounded, graceful, and compassionate facilitation to inspire transformation and liberation at the personal and collective levels. She has written several books: Pagan Portals (*Reclaiming Witchcraft* – 2020, *Aphrodite* – 2020, *Iris* – 2021, *Norns* – 2023, *Artemis* – 2024); Earth Spirit (*Honoring the Wild* – 2023, *Gaia* – 2023); and *Practically Pagan: An Alternative Guide to Health & Well-being* – 2020. Plus, she has written articles, blogs, and essays for Witches & Pagans, Pagan Dawn, Coreopsis Journal, Moon Books, Revelore Press, Llewellyn, Epona Muse Publishing, and more. In 2023, they self-published a book of poetry, *wrecked: the insistence of grief.* Irisanya cultivates spaces of self-care/devotion, divine relationship (whatever that means to you), and community service as part of her heart magick and activism. www.irisanyamoon.com

Frances Billinghurst is an initiated witch, magical practitioner and metaphysician who has been fascinated with mythology, folklore and esoteric sciences for over half her lifetime.

A prolific writer, Frances is the author of *Dancing the Sacred Wheel* (one of the few books solely dedicated to the sabbats in the Southern Hemisphere), *Encountering the Dark Goddess: A Journey into the Shadow Realms, Contemporary Witchcraft: Foundational Practices for a Magical Life* and *On Her Silver Rays: A Guide to the Moon, Myth and Magic* amongst other titles. She is the editor of *Call of the God: An Anthology Exploring the Divine Masculine within Modern Paganism,* and her essays have appeared in numerous publications over the years. Frances offers online courses through Udemy, has her own YouTube and can be found in several platforms. (Facebook and IG, https://mysticalsoulacademy.com or https://francesbillinghurst.blogspot.com.au).

Tiffany Lazic is a Registered Psychotherapist, Spiritual Director, and Certified Havening Techniques Practitioner, specializing in Spiritual Psychotherapy, with over two decades experience in individual, couples, and group therapy. Tiffany has a Bachelor's Degree (with Honours) in Film Studies from Ryerson University and is a graduate of the Transformational Arts College of Spiritual and Holistic Training's Spiritual Psychotherapy Training and Spiritual Directorship Training Programs. She taught in both training programs, served as supervisor for student psychotherapists, and taught all ten courses in the College's Discovering the Total Self Program. She also developed and taught courses for the College's Esoteric Studies Program. Tiffany created, edited, and published the online magazine, The Glowing Hive, from December 2011 to November 2013. Tiffany is the author of, *The Great Work: Self-Knowledge and Healing Through the Wheel of the Year* (Llewellyn Worldwide, May 2015) and *The Noble Art: From Shadow to Essence Through the Wheel of the Year* (Llewellyn Worldwide, October 2021). She is the originator of Hynni Energy Healing which is outlined in both her books. She has contributed to many books and annuals from various publishers and joyfully collaborated with talented designer, Esther Sanchez on *The Soul Alchemist Journal* (Gilded Peacock, November 2021). An international presenter, keynote speaker and retreat facilitator, Tiffany has conducted workshops for many conferences and organizations in Canada, the US, Mexico, India and the UK. She was one of the co-creators and co-organizers of Kitchener's SPARKS Symposium (2010 – 2012).

Annwyn Avalon is a Water Priestess and Water Witch with over 10 years of Water Priestess experience and over 15 years of Priestess and Magical experience. She is the founder of Triskele Rose, an Avalonian witchcraft tradition, and the 9 Month Water Magic course, which is the first of its kind covering all types of Water Magic, Witchcraft, and Priestess Practices. This course is offered once a year starting March 1st. She has devoted her life as a Priestess to the path of water, which is expressed through the study and creation of art, witchcraft, temple arts, dance, and water magic. She has a BFA in sculpture and a BA in anthropology and has completed her Reiki Master teacher training and studied herbalism and Middle Eastern folk and esoteric dancing. Annwyn is the author of *Water Witchcraft: Magic and Lore from the Celtic Tradition, The Way of the Water Priestess: Entering the World of Water magic,* and *The Celtic Goddess Grimoire.* She also writes the Patheos.com blog, The Water Witch, and is an award-winning, internationally-known dancer with a repertoire of water and mermaid-themed belly dance performances. Visit her at www.WaterPriestess.com waterwitchcraft.com and TriskeleRose.com for more information.

Sian Sibley is an animist witch and the author of *Unveiling the Green,* a book on working psychologically, alchemically, and astrologically with plant spirits. Sian's second book has just recently been released and is called *Black Paths and Green Cathedrals – Ecological Witchcraft.* This new book details Sian's passion for the ecology of our pagan practice and how we interact with the other inhabitants of the land. Sian is the Leader of the DragonOak coven and has over 30 years of practical witchcraft experience. She holds an MSc in Applied Biology and Medical Genetics and is currently studying for an MA in Ecology and Spirituality at the University of Wales, Trinity St Davids. Sian's perspective as a witch who is also a scientist gives her a unique perspective on the worlds of ecology, science, and their relationship to the magical world.

Rachel Patterson. Witch. Best Selling Author. Podcast Host. High Priestess. Speaker. Blogger. Writer. Reiki Master Certified Crystal Therapist. I am an English witch who has been walking the Pagan pathway for over thirty years. A working wife and mother who has been lucky enough to have had over 25 books published (so far), some of them becoming best sellers. My passion is to learn, I love to study and have done so from books, online resources, schools and wonderful mentors over the years and still continue to learn each and every day but I have learnt the most from actually getting outside and doing it. Host of the Pagan Portal Podcast, produced by Moon Books Publishing and released twice a month on the Moon Books YouTube channel and all your usual podcast providers, such as Spotify. It is my pleasure to give talks to pagan groups and co-run open rituals and workshops run by the Kitchen Witch Coven. High Priestess of the Kitchen Witch Coven and an Elder at the online Kitchen Witch School of Natural Witchcraft. A regular columnist with Fate & Fortune magazine, I also contribute articles to several magazines such as Pagan Dawn and Witchcraft & Wicca. You will find my regular ramblings on my own personal blog and YouTube channel. My craft is a combination of old religion witchcraft, Wicca, hedge witchery, kitchen witchery and folk magic. My heart is that of an English Kitchen Witch. It was my honour to be added to the Watkins 'Spiritual 100 List' for 2023.

Ness Bosch, La Huesera, is an Iberian Shamaness and Priestess. Author and independent researcher, mother of three, Ness lives in Scotland where she is a founding member of the Goddess Community Scotland. Founder of The Path of the Bones and the Clan of the Bone Woman (La Huesera), she shares the teachings of this path with those ready to move on into advanced animistic ways of working in the realms, with the spirits and teaches the ways of shadowhunting. She is the Head of the Covenant of the Waters and the Temple of Astarte. Before moving to Scotland, Ness was a Regional Coordinator for the Pagan Federation International in Spain. She is a Hierophant Priestess, Dame Commander, and Archdruidess of the Fellowship of Isis. Ness holds a seat in the Pagan Heathen Symposium.

Victoria Scobie is a General Practitioner (Family Doctor) and Educator from Ayrshire, Scotland who has lived both in the United Kingdon and New Zealand. She also studied English Literature and enjoys exploring Celtic Mythology as part of a more Holistic approach to health where stories can be used as medicine. Victoria enjoys helping others navigate their own healing pathway – incorporating logical, left brain-approaches found in mainstream healthcare systems, plus more creative and symbolic right-brain approaches. This led to her training with Ness Bosch as a shamanic practitioner, plus upskilling in trauma-informed practices, somatic work, Mind-Body Medicine and Acceptance and Commitment therapy (ACT).

Monica Gobbin is a Pedagog and Researcher in Educational Issues. During her training as a Priestess of the Goddess, she built her work as a therapist by uniting different tools. Shamanic Techniques, Crystals… She is a Tarot reader and one of the most respectable Astrologers of the Spanish Speaking Pagan Community. She is also a floral therapist, Reiki Master, Magnified Healing Master and trained with Dr. J. L. Cabouli on past life regression therapy. She is the High Priestess of the Goddess of the Southern Cross community and the author of *Dancing the Mandala of your Moons*.

Isabel Alameda Jaut graduated in Psychology with a firm conviction to dedicate herself to helping therapeutically. Over the years, she has worked intensively in therapeutic processes with many people, accompanying them on their path to well-being and self-knowledge. Her interest in her spiritual growth led her to delve into other subjects such as astrology, and therapeutic tarot… To finally integrate them into her professional practice and be able to offer a more comprehensive approach. This combination of disciplines allows her to guide women not only in their personal development but also in their spiritual growth. Her love for learning and her curiosity for anthropology and ethnography have led Isabel to study and document different traditions and spiritual practices from various cultures. And she uses different digital resources to provide accessible and practical tools that promote comprehensive well-being, from a respectful and sensitive approach. Instagram @psiquedelaluna

Lindsay River is a poet and writer who studies mythology, primarily of Mesopotamia and of Wales and Ireland. She has been a devotee of Inanna since 1982 and has worked for many years on the relation of Her mythology to the cycles of the planet Venus. She has worked as an astrologer and a homoeopath and for social justice. In 1987 she published, with Sally Gillespie, *The Knot of Time: astrology and female experience*. She has been an activist on LGBTQIA rights since 1972. She loves queerness, flights of imagination, the Hag of Wookey Hole, caves, Welsh countryside and culture, animals, birds and insects, minerals, wild plants, embroidery and other crafts, rare books, vintage objects, subtle colours and deep friendships.

Mael Brigde is the author of *A Brigit of Ireland Devotional – Sun Among Stars*, a collection of contemplative poetry, essays and resources. She is a devotee of Brigit and the founder of Daughters of the Flame, which has tended Brigit's flame since Imbolc 1993. Unknown to them for several years, on that same day in Ireland Catholic Brigidine Sisters were also relighting her Flame. Mael Brigde publishes two Brigit blogs, Brigit's Sparkling Flame, and Stone on the Belly (poetry). Her reviews of Brigit-related books are gathered in her paper, A Long Sip at the Well and "The Mythical Pairing of Brig and Bres" discusses Brigit as sovereignty goddess. She teaches courses and webinars on Brigit, including Journey with Brigit, Goddess of Poetry, an intensive class that explores reading and writing poetry as a sacred act, offering meditations, historical information, and the model of ancient and modern Irish poets. Mael Brigde lives in Vancouver, Canada. Website https://bit.ly/MaelBrigde

Emily Carding is an experienced Shakespearean actor, having appeared in versions of over twenty of Shakespeare's plays, both on stage and screen. They hold a BA (hons) in Theatre Arts from Bretton Hall and an MFA in Staging Shakespeare from the University of Exeter. Emily is also an accomplished screen actor, and played opposite Martin Freeman in the British horror movie hit, *Ghost Stories* and will appear on cinema screens in 2024 as Dara in *Return to Silent Hill* directed by Christophe Gans. Emily is also a published creator of a number of highly popular Tarot decks including The Transparent Tarot, The Transparent Oracle and Tarot of the Sidhe, and author of esoteric works, including *Faery Craft*, (Llewellyn 2012) *So Potent Art: The Magic of Shakespeare* (Llewellyn 2021) and *Seeking Faery* (Llewellyn 2022) Emily Carding believe in making hidden wisdom accessible and enjoyable to all who seek knowledge, always hoping to inspire, educate and initiate.

MOON BOOKS
PAGANISM & SHAMANISM

What is Paganism? A religion, a spirituality, an alternative belief system, nature worship? You can find support for all these definitions (and many more) in dictionaries, encyclopaedias, and text books of religion, but subscribe to any one and the truth will evade you. Above all Paganism is a creative pursuit, an encounter with reality, an exploration of meaning and an expression of the soul. Druids, Heathens, Wiccans and others, all contribute their insights and literary riches to the Pagan tradition. Moon Books invites you to begin or to deepen your own encounter, right here, right now.

If you have enjoyed this book, why not tell other readers by posting a review on your preferred book site.

Bestsellers from Moon Books

Keeping Her Keys
An Introduction to Hekate's Modern Witchcraft
Cyndi Brannen
Blending Hekate, witchcraft and personal development
together to create a powerful new magickal perspective.
Paperback: 978-1-78904-075-3 ebook 978-1-78904-076-0

Journey to the Dark Goddess
How to Return to Your Soul
Jane Meredith
Discover the powerful secrets of the Dark Goddess and
transform your depression, grief and pain into healing
and integration.
Paperback: 978-1-84694-677-6 ebook: 978-1-78099-223-5

Shamanic Reiki
Expanded Ways of Working with Universal Life Force Energy
Llyn Roberts, Robert Levy
Shamanism and Reiki are each powerful ways of healing; together,
their power multiplies. Shamanic Reiki introduces techniques to
help healers and Reiki practitioners tap ancient healing wisdom.
Paperback: 978-1-84694-037-8 ebook: 978-1-84694-650-9

Southern Cunning
Folkloric Witchcraft in the American South
Aaron Oberon
Modern witchcraft with a Southern flair, this book is a
journey through the folklore of the American South and
a look at the power these stories hold for modern witches.
Paperback: 978-1-78904-196-5 ebook: 978-1-78904-197-2

Bestsellers from Moon Books
Pagan Portals Series

The Morrigan
Meeting the Great Queens

Morgan Daimler

Ancient and enigmatic, the Morrigan reaches out to us.
On shadowed wings and in raven's call, meet the ancient Irish
goddess of war, battle, prophecy, death, sovereignty, and magic.

Paperback: 978-1-78279-833-0 ebook: 978-1-78279-834-7

The Awen Alone
Walking the Path of the Solitary Druid

Joanna van der Hoeven

An introductory guide for the solitary Druid, The Awen Alone
will accompany you as you explore, and seek out your
own place within the natural world.

Paperback: 978-1-78279-547-6 ebook: 978-1-78279-546-9

Moon Magic
Rachel Patterson

An introduction to working with the phases of the Moon,
what they are and how to live in harmony with the lunar
year and to utilise all the magical powers it provides.

Paperback: 978-1-78279-281-9 ebook: 978-1-78279-282-6

Hekate
A Devotional

Vivienne Moss

Hekate, Queen of Witches and the Shadow-Lands,
haunts the pages of this devotional bringing magic
and enchantment into your lives.

Paperback: 978-1-78535-161-7 ebook: 978-1-78535-162-4

Readers of ebooks can buy or view any of these bestsellers by clicking on the live link in the title. Most titles are published in paperback and as an ebook. Paperbacks are available in traditional bookshops. Both print and ebook formats are available online.

Find more titles and sign up to our readers' newsletter www.collectiveinkbooks.com/paganism

For video content, author interviews and more, please subscribe to our YouTube channel.

MoonBooksPublishing

Follow us on social media for book news, promotions and more:

Facebook: Moon Books

Instagram: @MoonBooksCI

X: @MoonBooksCI

TikTok: @MoonBooksCI

Printed and bound by CPI Group (UK) Ltd, Croydon, CR0 4YY

27/10/2025

01985978-0001